RIBCHESTER EXCAVATIONS

Part 3

Excavations in the Civil Settlement

1968-1980

B. Pottery & Coins

Editors:

B.J.N.Edwards   P.V.Webster

With Contributions By:

P.Gibbons, K.F.Hartley, L.Hird,

J.Patterson, R.C.Turner, D.C.A.Shotter,

F.C.Wild, J.H.S.Witherington.

UNIVERSITY COLLEGE, CARDIFF,

DEPARTMENT OF

EXTRA-MURAL STUDIES

1988

ISBN   0 946045 31 3

Produced by the Archaeology Research Fund of the Department of
Extra-Mural Studies, University College, Cardiff with the aid of a
grant from the Historic Buildings & Monuments Commission (England).

Enquiries concerning the purchase of this volume should be made to:

The Administrative Officer,
Department of Extra-Mural Studies
University College
38 Park Place
CARDIFF CF1 3BB

Or:

The County Archaeologist
Lancashire Record Office
Bow Lane
PRESTON PR1 2RE

LIST OF CONTENTS

LIST OF ILLUSTRATIONS

PREFACE

This third part of the several-part publication of recent excavations at Ribchester will appear at the same time as the second part in the series and is dependent upon it. It sets out the essential dating evidence for the structures in the civil settlement, separated here, for ease of reference, into three long chapters according to the class of find. Our debt to individuals and institutions has been detailed in part 2. Pagination, chapter and find numbers start afresh in this part so that, if preferred, the part may be used on its own.

Chapter 1
THE SAMIAN WARE
By Felicity Wild

The pottery described below is divided according to site, in the order in which it appears in the 'structural' reports in part 2 of this series. Bibliography and abbreviations appear at the end of this volume.

I should like to express my grateful thanks to B.R.Hartley and Brenda Dickinson of Leeds University, both for their assistance in finding parallels to individual decorated sherds and for providing detailed identifications of the potters' stamps. The potter and die numbers are theirs (potter numbers are in lower case Roman numerals to distinguish their numbering system from that of Stanfield and Simpson for Central Gaul and Ricken for Rheinzabern, both of whom use upper case Roman numerals) and will appear in their forthcoming index of potters' stamps on samian ware. According to their notation [1] placed after the name of a pottery denotes that the stamp in question has been recorded there, [2] that other stamps of the same potter have been recorded there and [3] that the stamp has been assigned to that pottery on the basis of form and fabric. The letter S after a catalogue entry indicates a potter's stamp.

a) The Playing Fields excavation, 1969.

i)Phase 2.

From levelling, below the floor of Building 3:
1.   Form 29, South Gaulish. Two fragments of the upper zone, showing a panel containing rows of horizontal wreaths and one containing the dog (0.1965) over chevrons. The dog was used by Frontinus and on a bowl from Pompeii by Rufinus (Atkinson 1914, pl.VI, 35, which also appears to show the same wreath). Rufinus also used the chevron (Knorr 1919, Taf.68, 19). c.A.D.70-85. 1.8.

From levelling, below Building 5:
2.   Form 30, South Gaulish, showing an ovolo with three-pronged terminal. Flavian or Trajanic. 1.8.

From levelling in trench 1 at datum 30-32 ft.
3.   Form 29, South Gaulish, slightly burnt. One fragment from the lower part of the bowl shows a festoon containing the triangular leaf used by many of the Flavian potters at La Graufesenque. The leaf occurs in a festoon on a form 29 by Secundus from Pompeii (Atkinson 1914, pl.V, 24). A bowl by Sabinus from Mainz (Knorr 1919, Taf.69B) shows it used similarly, inside a triple festoon, on the lower part of the lower zone, as on the Ribchester piece. c.A.D.70-85. 1.8b.

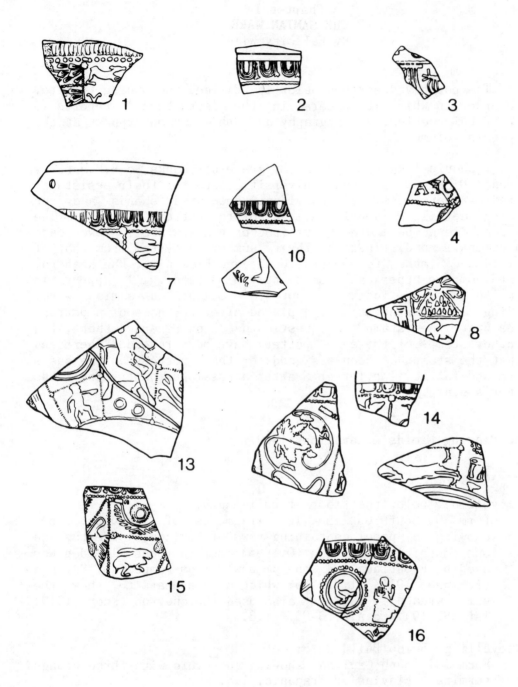

Fig.1. Samian nos. 1-16. Scale 1:2.

From the demolition debris of Building 7:

4.(S) Form 37, Central Gaulish. One fragment, burnt, showing the lower edge of the decoration, bordered by a bead row, containing the large stamp OF.ATT (ret), die 4a of Attianus ii of Lezoux [1]. c.A.D.125-145. 1.44.

From pit 2.16a:

5.(S) Form 27, East Gaulish, stamped S IIXTVS⊢, die 1a of the potter Sextus iii. This stamp, quite unlike any other from an East Gaulish Sextus, has been recorded from Xanten, Tongres and Mainz-Weisenau, also on form 27. As this form ceases to be made after the early Antonine period, the stamp is likely to be of Hadrianic or early Antonine date. 2.16a.

From the levelling over pit 2.16a:

6.(S) Form 18/31, Central Gaulish. Half the bowl, stamped SENONIO, die 3a of the potter Senonius. Senonius, who appears to have been a Central Gaulish potter, although there is no evidence for the exact location of his factory, worked in the Antonine period. 2.16.

From the upper levels of a pit:

7. Form 37, South Gaulish. Two fragments showing a Flavian-Trajanic three-pronged ovolo. The decoration is in panels, one of which contains the hare (O.2129). This type was used by the potters whose work occurs in the Bregenz Cellar Find (Jacobs 1912, Taf.II, 9, 10). The bowl has been broken and rivetted together in antiquity. One fragment contains parts of three lead rivets, the other one rivet hole. c.A.D. 90-110. 2.15.

From levels probably contemporary with Phase 2:

8. Form 37, South Gaulish. One fragment with very poorly impressed decoration showing panels. These show, on the left a column and arcade, on the right a cross ornament with leaf tips in the lower zone, over a hare (possibly O.2107, used by Frontinus and Germanus). The cross ornament with leaf-tip filling can be paralleled on a sherd from Holt dated to the Domitianic-Trajanic period (Grimes 1930, fig.38, 60). The detail of the column is not clear, but arcade decoration of this type occurs at Bregenz (Jacobs 1912, Taf.III, 18) and on bowls in the style of Mascuus (Knorr 1952, Taf.37C, D). It is unlikely from the shape that this is a Mascuus column. c.A.D.90-110. 4.5.

ii) **Phase** 3.

From the roadway:

9.(S) Form 18/31, Central Gaulish. Almost half the bowl stamped MEDETI.M, die 3a of Medetus of Les Martres-de-Veyre [1]. c.A.D.100-120. 1.43.

From the destruction of Building 10 or levelling for Building 11:

10.   Form 37, Central Gaulish. Two fragments, burnt, in the style of Albucius. One fragment has his ovolo; the other the lower edge of the decoration, which is clearly from a freestyle bowl, with leaf tips in the field characteristic of Albucius' work (S&S, pl.123, passim.). The type is probably the bear (O.1608) also used by him. c.A.D. 150-180. 2.18.

From levelling probably associated with Building 13:

11.(S) Form 81, Central Gaulish, stamped •PATER[ΛTIΘF], die 1a of Pateratus of Lezoux [1], on the upper part of the wall. Stamps of Pateratus on form 81 have also been recorded from Corbridge and Richborough. c.A.D.150-180. 2.64.

iii) Plain ware.

A list of plain samian from stratified contexts will be placed in the site archive. Where relevant, individual pieces are mentioned in the structural reports (Part 2 of this series, Chapter 2).

iv) Unstratified samian.

A detailed list of all decorated sherds from unstratified contexts and a summary of the plain ware will be placed in the site archive. Apart from the single stamp and four pieces of intrinsic interest published below, the only piece to merit mention was one of form Ritterling 12. This normally pre-Flavian form was thought to have been superceded by Curle 11 by c.A.D.70. However, a number of examples have been found on fort sites of presumed Agricolan origin in the North of Britain. A second example from Ribchester is in the Ribchester Museum and others are known from Melandra, Ebchester and the Agricolan fort at Cardean in Scotland.

12.(S) Form 18 or 15/17, South Gaulish, stamped OF.CΛ[L.VI], die 5z of Calvus i of La Graufesenque [2]. c.A.D. 65-80.

13.   Form 37, Central Gaulish. Two joining fragments showing panel decoration with the finely beaded borders used by Donnaucus and Ioenalis and their associates at Les Martres-de-Veyre, and, at a slightly later period, by Birrantus and Drusus II at Lezoux. The panels contain the pigmy (O.692), the seated Apollo (O.83) and probably the lion (O.1504). Bowls in this style have been attributed to the styles of Donnaucus and Ioenalis since, of the Trajanic and early Hadrianic potters who made them, only these two potters appear to have signed their work. The fabric of the bowl suggests an origin at Lezoux rather than at Les Martres-de-Veyre. It is known that, during the early Hadrianic period, potters at Lezoux were producing bowls in a similar style to those at Les Martres, but these bowls,

too, tend not to be signed by their makers. c.A.D. 100-125 (although if this is, indeed, a Lezoux product, its date is likely to be c.A.D.120-130).

14.   Form 37, Central Gaulish. Five fragments including one of base, probably all from the same bowl, in the same fabric and style as no.13 above. Two sherds show traces of lead rivets, where the bowl has been mended in antiquity. The ovolo is that found on bowls in the 'Donnaucus-Ioenalis' style (S&S, pl.49, 578). The pedestal ornament is that illustrated on a bowl from London (S&S, pl.48, 567), which also appears on a signed bowl of Drusus II (S&S, pl.89, 16). The dog (O.1979) was used, among other potters, by Ioenalis. c.A.D. 100-125, or more probably c.A.D. 120-130.

15.   Form 37, Central Gaulish. One fragment showing panels containing a cross motif and festoon with beaded ring over the hare (O.2057). Although the ovolo is not one commonly used by them and the borders are of larger beads, this piece clearly has affinities with the style of the 'Donnaucus-Ioenalis' group. The hare was used by these potters; the festoon and beaded ring are among their characteristic details. The cross design is not unlike that on a sherd from Brecon in 'Donnaucus style' (S&S, pl.49, 588), although the detail differs slightly. The fabric appears to be that of Lezoux. The date is almost certainly c.A.D.120-130.

16.   Form 37, East Gaulish. Two joining fragments in the fabric and style of the potteries at La Madeleine. The ovolo appears to be Ricken's ovolo B; the decoration shows a medallion (Ricken 1934, Taf.IX, 9) containing the bird (ibid. Taf.VII, 111: O.2301), the figure to the left (ibid. Taf.IX, 15: O.923c) and the draped woman (ibid. Taf.VII, 97: O.939A). Beneath is a wreath of the fleur-de-lys, Ricken 1934, 11. The decoration can be paralleled almost exactly on sherds cited by Ricken from Zugmantel (ibid., 140); Z438, with his ovolo B, shows the medallion (O.939a) and the same basal wreath; Z437, with his ovolo C, shows the medallion containing the same bird, and both the other figure types. Ricken considered that pieces in this style were contemporary with those found in the earth and timber fort at Saalburg, now thought to end shortly before A.D.139 (Schonberger 1969, 165, n.164). If this dating is correct, the Ribchester piece is likely to be Hadrianic or early Antonine.

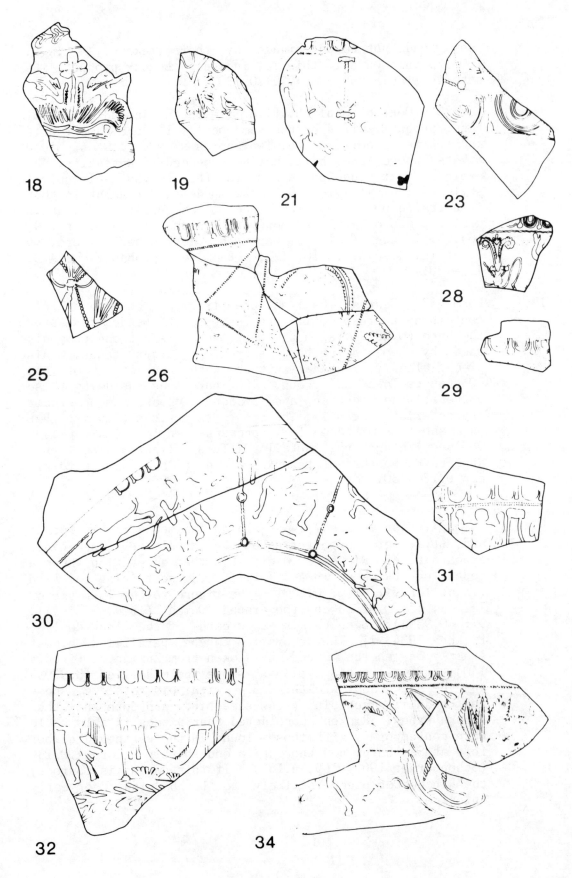

Fig.2. Samian nos. 18–34. Scale 1:2.

b) **Sewerage Scheme, 1976.**

Comparatively little material from the excavation and watching brief was well stratified. A summary of all the samian from stratified groups will be placed in the site archive and is the source of details of dating given in part 2 of this series. All the stamps and significant decorated pieces are listed below, arranged in Field number order. Unstratified stamps and a selection of decorated ware are listed at the end, for the light that they shed on the range of wares and the dating of the site as a whole.

i) **Cutting I.**

Pit FN1:

17.(S)   Form 15/17 or 18, South Gaulish, stamped LOGIRN[I], die 5a of Logirnus of La Graufesenque [1]. This is one of Logirnus' latest stamps, which occurs at Camelon (twice) and Inchtuthil (four times). It is also known from Risstissen. c.A.D.75–90.   AO.

The latest piece from FN1 was a Central Gaulish scrap of Hadrianic or early Antonine date (CY)

From lower levels, section 1, FN2:

18.   Form 37, East Gaulish, in the style of Reginus I of Rheinzabern. The decoration shows the palmette (Ricken & Fischer 1963, type P.50) with a small leaf (ibid.P.81) above it. Both occur at Rheinzabern in the style of Reginus I (Ricken 1948, taf.18, 1,6 for P.50, taf.18, 4 for P.81) although not together, as here. He also used the wreath motif (Ricken & Fischer 1963, R.2) in place of the ovolo (Ricken 1948, taf.18, 15–17, 19).   c.A.D.160–200.

ii) **Cutting II.**

Pit FN243: from the upper layers of the pit (D):

19.   Form 37, Central Gaulish. One fragment of scroll bowl with bird (O.2298) and leaf. The leaf was used by Attianus (S&S, pl.87, 21) and is the same as that used on no.48 below, by an anonymous potter connected with the Sacer group. c.A.D.130–160.   EH.

Material from lower layers was all South Gaulish and Flavian. It included:

20.(S)   Form 15/17R, South Gaulish, stamped OFBAS[SI.CO], die 5b of the Bassus i –Coelus association of La Graufesenque [1]. The stamp appears chiefly on rouletted dishes, but is also occasionally used on form 29, with decoration typical of the Neronian period. The site record includes Risstissen and Ubbergen. c.A.D. 55–70. EI.

iii) **Cutting III.**

Well FN300 with material of early Antonine date:
21.   Form 37, Central Gaulish. One fragment showing a rivet hole
         and part of a lead rivet. The decoration, which is poorly
         impressed, as if the bowl had been made in a worn or dirty
         mould, is in the style of Docilis. It shows panels with Pan
         (O.717) impressed twice and an uncertain type, possibly
         Mercury (O.538A). The ovolo occurs on bowls signed by
         Docilis from Poitiers and Mumrills; see also a sherd from
         the 1970 excavations at Ribchester, Edwards & Webster 1985,
         no.60. c.A.D.140-160.   AG.

FN317, in a Trajanic to early Antonine group:
22.(S)   Form 18/31, Central Gaulish, stamped OVIDI.M, die 1c
         probably of Ovidius of Les Martres-de-Veyre [2]. The stamp
         has not been recorded before, and is in Lezoux fabric, but
         it is likely to be the work of the same potter and suggests
         that he may have migrated to Lezoux. His other stamps are
         known from Corbridge and the deposits from the London
         second fire. c.A.D. 115-135.   BW.

Occupation material FN321:
23.   Form 37, South Gaulish, showing panel decoration over a
         zone of triple festoons. A similar zone of double festoons
         with the same pendant occurs on two bowls from Ovilava
         attributed to the style of Vitalis (Karnitsch 1959, Taf.9,
         8, 9), while triple festoons with birds occur on bowls in
         the style of Mercato (ibid., Taf.14, 4-6). An identical
         festoon with the bud from the upper zone occurs on a bowl
         from Gloucester, where it appears with a zone of decoration
         precisely paralleled on a bowl stamped by M.Crestio. The
         zonal scheme and parallels to the work of Flavian potters
         suggest a date c.A.D. 80-100.   EM.

         Three sherds (from AC, AH) were associated with this
         context. None need be later than the Hadrianic period. From
         AC:

24.(S)   Form 33, Central Gaulish, stamped VIDVC[OS.F], die 4a of
         Viducus of Les Martres-de-Veyre [1]. The stamp occurs in
         groups from the Hadrianic fire of London. c.A.D. 105-125.
         AC.

25.   Form 37, Central Gaulish, showing part of a saltire
         ornament. The potter is uncertain, but the light fabric and
         seven-beaded rosette in the centre both suggest a
         Hadrianic-early Antonine date.   AC.

iv) **Cutting I extension.**

FN501:
26.　　　Form 37, Central Gaulish. Five fragments from a bowl with
　　　　　ovolo (Rogers B.20) used by Secundinus i. The decoration
　　　　　shows saltire motifs and an arcade containing Venus
　　　　　(0.278). The arcade (Rogers F.41) is a common feature of
　　　　　Secundinus' work (cf. Rogers & Laing 1966, pl.III, 59). The
　　　　　supporting motif (Rogers G.233), saltire and trifid bud
　　　　　(ibid. G.18) and leaf (ibid.H.153), and basal wreath (ibid.
　　　　　G.287) all occur on a bowl in his style from Alchester
　　　　　(Hawkes 1927, fig.5, 6). The occurrence of this potter's
　　　　　work at Carzield in Dumfrieshire and also in the Birdoswald
　　　　　Alley (Richmond & Birley 1930, fig.3) suggests a date
　　　　　c.A.D. 125-150.　　(FE, FG, AK).

FN505: a mid second century group. The latest sherds include form
　　　　　37, showing Cinnamus' ovolo 2 (c.A.D. 150-170) and a
　　　　　fragment of form 18/31R or 31R (probably an early version
　　　　　of 31R) datable to c.A.D.150.

27.(S)　Form 33, Central Gaulish, stamped [C]RACVNA.F, die 2a of
　　　　　Cracuna i of Lezoux [1]. This stamp is rather more common
　　　　　in Antonine Scotland than at sites on Hadrian's Wall. It
　　　　　has also been noted at Verulamium (Period IIb, before
　　　　　c.A.D. 140) but occurs in a pit dated to the 150's at
　　　　　Alcester. It appears frequently on forms 18/31 and 27.
　　　　　c.A.D. 130-160.　FI.

28.　　　Form 37, Central Gaulish, showing panels with saltire and
　　　　　slave (0.647). The style is that of one of the mould-makers
　　　　　associated with Donnaucus' style (termed X-13 by Rogers)
　　　　　who used the ovolo and borders (S&S, pl.47, 549) and the
　　　　　ramshorns (S&S, pl.48, 568). The fabric could be that of
　　　　　Les Martres-de-Veyre, suggesting a date c.A.D. 100-125.
　　　　　FI.

FN507: a Hadrianic or early Antonine group.
29.　　　Form 37, Central Gaulish. One fragment showing ovolo and
　　　　　wreath of chevrons. The ovolo is probably that used by
　　　　　Stanfield's X-6 (S&S, pl.74). Horizontal wreaths of rather
　　　　　larger chevrons occur on bowls with different ovolos
　　　　　attributed to his style (S&S, pl.76, 23) and a date in the
　　　　　Hadrianic or early Antonine period seems probable.　FK.

v) **Cutting IV.**

Slot FN613:
30.　　　Form 37, Central Gaulish. Two fragments with poorly applied
　　　　　and abraded panel decoration with a lion (0.1439), hound
　　　　　(0.1980), warrior (uncertain), figure (0.684, probably a
　　　　　flute player) and animals, probably a lion and stag, over
　　　　　hares (0.2059, 0.2116). The style is that of the

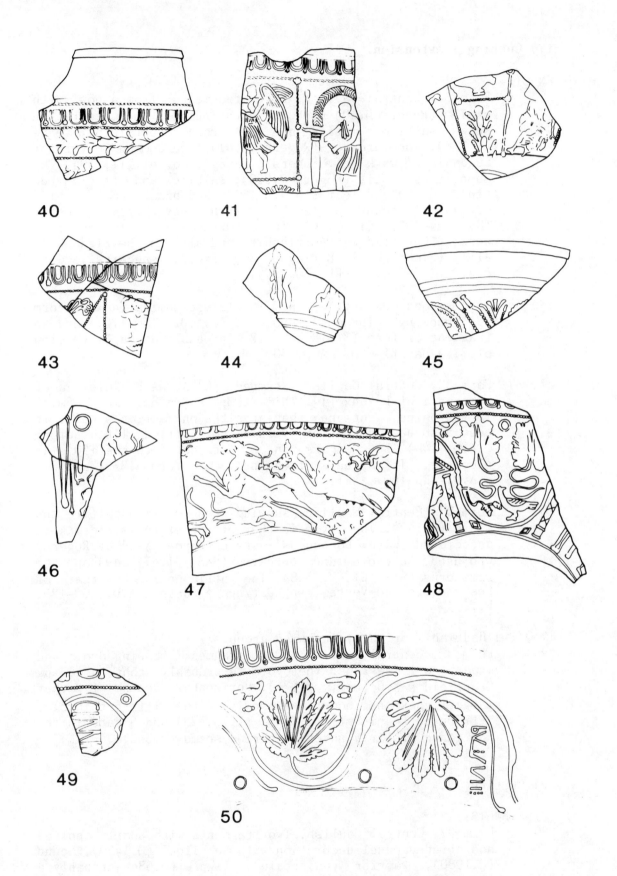

Fig.3. Samian nos. 40–50. Scale 1:2.

Quintilianus group. The ovolo and wavy lines occur on a bowl in the London Museum, signed by Bassus. The double basal ridge is also a feature of the Quintilianus Group style. c.A.D. 125-150.   GK.

Hollow FN633. The latest sherd in the group is:
31.   Form 37, Central Gaulish, in the style of Cinnamus, showing his ovolo 3 and Perseus (O.234). c.A.D. 150-170.   HC.

FN637:
32.   Form 37, South Gaulish. Abraded panel decoration shows Victory (O.808B) and an uncertain type over festoons with a bird (O.2247). The style is that of a group of late Flavian-Trajanic potters, including Mascuus, whose work is common in Britain and can be dated from its occurrence in the Bregenz Cellar deposit. The corner leaf is typical of their work. The victory, ovolo and basal wreath occur together on a bowl in this style from Northwich (Wild 1971, fig.15B). All these features can be paralleled on bowls from Bregenz (Jacobs 1912, 7, 13). c.A.D. 90-110.   HA.

vi) Area E.

FN700, layer 3 , a Hadrianic-early Antonine group:
33.(S) Form 18/31, Central Gaulish, stamped [PA]TER.F, die 2a of Pater ii of Lezoux [1]. This stamp has been found at Lezoux in a large pit group of c.A.D.135-145. It is also known from the Antonine fort at Newstead and the Saalburg Erdkastell. c.A.D. 130-150.   GR.

34.   Form 37, Central Gaulish. Seven fragments of scroll bowl with birds (O.2252), showing sphinxes (O.852, O.856) beneath an uncertain animal in the lower concavities. A bowl in the style of Attianus from the Birdoswald Alley shows the same general scheme, with the sphinxes, leaf-tip filling ornament, birds and similar animal in the upper panel (S&S, pl.87, 20). The leaves are Rogers H.58, which was used by Attianus and ibid. J.56. The ovolo is Attianus' ovolo 1 (S&S, fig.23, 1). c.A.D.130-160.   GR.

vii) Unstratified.

The stamps are listed in alphabetical order, the decorated ware chronologically.

35.(S) Form 18/31R, Central Gaulish, stamped BO [OXS.F:.], die 3c of Bonoxus. Although Bonoxus is known to have worked at Lezoux, where he made form 80, though rarely, the majority of his stamps have been noted as in the fabric of Les Martres-de-Veyre and he probably only moved to Lezoux at the end of his career. This particular stamp is in the same style as ones assigned on fabric to Les Martres. It occurs in the Saalburg Erdkastell. c.A.D. 120-135. BV.

36.(S) Form 33, Central Gaulish, stamped [CA]NA.I.M, die 1a of Canaus of Lezoux [1]. The dating evidence for this potter rests mainly on his forms, which include 18/31, 27 and 80. His work occurs occasionally in Lower Germany, suggesting some activity before A.D.150 and there is one stamp from Malton. c.A.D. 140-170. HG.

37.(S) Form 33, Central Gaulish, stamped CEL IANI.M, die 3b of Celsianus of Lezoux [2]. This is an uncommon stamp of which the only other example comes from Lisieux. Since his work is common at sites in the North of Britain reoccupied or founded c.A.D. 160 and he regularly made forms 31R, 79 and 80, his range will have been c.A.D. 160-190. HE.

38.(S) Form 33, Central Gaulish, stamped REBVRRIOF. The potter is Reburrus ii of Lezoux, though the stamp is so eroded that the precise die is uncertain. Reburrus' work appears in early to mid-Antonine contexts at Lezoux. His record includes sites in northern Britain reoccupied c.A.D.160, but, as his stamps are fairly common on form 27, his range is probably c.A.D. 140-170. CU.

39.(S) Form 31, Central Gaulish, stamped [REBV]RRIM, die 11a of Reburrus ii of Lezoux [1]. This stamp occurs mainly on form 27. Cf. no.38 above. c.A.D. 140-170. HE.

40. Form 37, South Gaulish, showing a single-bordered ovolo with rosette tongue and a straight wreath of trifid leaves, bordered by bead rows. The same features occur on a bowl from Period IB-C at Fishbourne (Dannell 1971, fig.128, 19) and the ovolo and beads, possibly with this wreath, on a bowl from a pit at Verulamium, filled by c.A.D. 75 (Hartley 1972, fig.86, 41). As these bowls are all of form 37, which was not commonly made before c.A.D.70, the probable date is c.A.D.70-90. AK.

41. Form 30, South Gaulish, in the style of a group of late Flavian-Trajanic potters including Mascuus. The Victory (O.808B) and leaf tuft occur on a bowl signed by Mascuus from Cannstatt (Knorr 1952, Taf.37B). The Peleus (O.883) with right hand broken was used by Mercato and occurs on a bowl in Mascuus' style (together with the column, arcade and leaf tuft) from the Bregenz Cellar deposit (Jacobs 1912, 7). c.A.D. 90-110. AK.

42. Form 37, South Gaulish, in the style of the same group if potters as no.41 above, showing a bird (O.2237) over a vertical wreath of leaf buds and an erotic group (O.P). All these features occur on a group of bowls in this style from Northwich (Wild 1971, fig.15, A-H); bowl D shows the same

group with a similarly-used vertical wreath, but without the other trifid bud commonly used by these potters. c.A.D. 90-110.   AJ.

43.   Form 37, Central Gaulish. Three fragments showing panel decoration with a saltire containing acanthus (Rogers 1974, K.2) and Jupiter (0.3). The fabric is probably that of Les Martres-de-Veyre and the style that of the Donnaucus-Ioenalis group, who used the acanthus and saltire (cf. S&S, pl.48, 562, 568).   c.A.D. 100-125.   GU.

44.   Form 64, Central Gaulish, in the light orange, micaceous fabric with dull orange 'glaze' typical of the pre-export period at Lezoux, but also sometimes occurring during the Hadrianic period, particularly on the rarer forms, such as this. The types are Venus (0.302) and Apollo (0.77). Both were used by Libertus, who also made this form. Trajanic or Hadrianic.   BV.

45.   Form 37, Central Gaulish. Two joining fragments showing decoration with festoon (Rogers F.41) and bud motif (ibid. G.8). The ovolo has been removed during the bowl-finishing process. In the absence of the ovolo, the potter remains uncertain. A Hadrianic or early Antonine date seems probable.   BZ.

46.   Form 37, Central Gaulish. Two joining fragments, showing abraded panel decoration with gadroon and Diana (0.106). The object at the edge of the right hand panel may be a worn label stamp. In length it matches the stamp ATTIANO of Attianus. The trilobed motif at the base of the bead row may be his (S&S, fig.23, 6). The piece is certainly Hadrianic or early Antonine and, if by Attianus, c.A.D. 130-160.   AA.

47.   Form 37, Central Gaulish, showing freestyle hunting scene with panther (0.1537), goat (0.1849) and small panther (0.1512). The snake-on-rock ornament and all the types were used by Attianus and, later, Criciro. The ovolo is probably that listed for Sacer (S&S, fig.22, 1) and the bowl is likely to be the work of the Sacer-Attianus group, c.A.D. 130-160.   BV.

48.   Form 37, Central Gaulish, showing scroll decoration with birds (0.2239B, 0.2295A) and in the lower concavities a shrine with erotic groups (0.B and 0.H). The distinctive ovolo (Rogers B.262) lacks an independent tongue, which takes the form of a blob attached to the right hand side of the egg, showing an X when clearly impressed. Although it is known on a number of bowls related to the Sacer-Attianus style, its user remains anonymous. A bowl from Little Chester (Hartley 1961, fig.7, 20) shows it with the groups 0.B and 0.H and one from Straubing (Walke 1965, taf.11, 3)

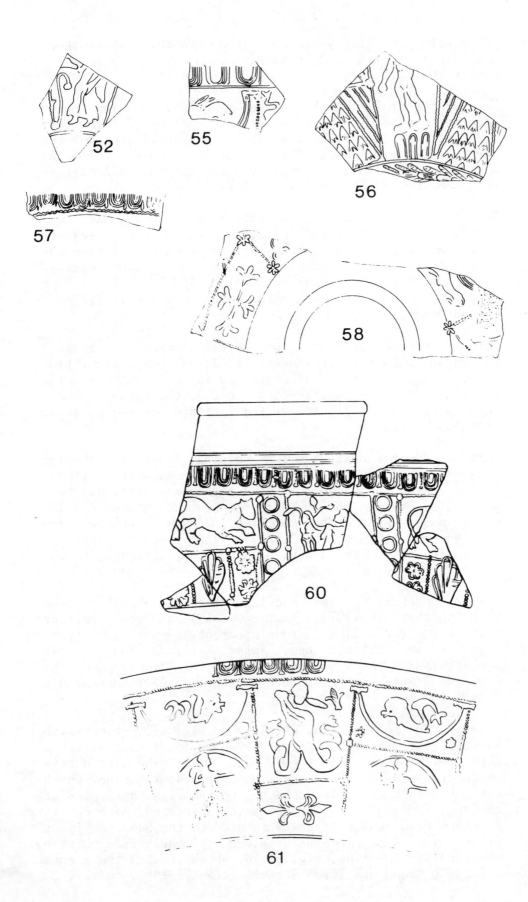

Fig.4. Samian nos. 52-61. Scale 1:2.

with a very similar scroll, with long tendrils ending in the same bud. The ovolo has also been noted in Antonine contexts in Scotland. The bowl also has affinities with Sacer, who used the shrine, Attianus, who used the leaf, and Cinnamus, who used several features. A date c.A.D. 130-160 seems probable. AB.

49.   Form 37, Central Gaulish, showing the large CINN[AMIO F] stamp, die 1a of Cinnamus ii of Lezoux. The ovolo is his ovolo 1 and the decoration probably shows an arcade supported by caryatids (O.1199). A bowl from Lezoux (S&S, pl.161, 47) shows the ovolo, stamp and arcades. c.A.D. 155-175. CU.

50.   Form 37, Central Gaulish. Many fragments of a bowl with the stamp PATERN[FE] (ret.), die 7a of Paternus v of Lezoux. The decoration shows a scroll with leaf (Rogers H.27) and peacock ((O.2365), which appears on a signed bowl with this ovolo from London (S&S, pl.107, 26). c.A.D. 160-200. DC.

c)   Sheltered Housing Accomodation, 1980

The excavations produced little samian ware and much of it was abraded. A summary of all stratified samian will be placed in the site archive. Stamps and diagnostic decorated sherds are listed below by period.

i) **Period 2.**   Earliest Roman Features.

The earliest material from these levels was Flavian, the latest probably Hadrianic. The material from the horizon contemporary with the early pits (66) was probably all of Flavian or Flavian-Trajanic date and included:

51.   (Not illustrated). Form 37, South Gaulish, showing ovolo and a zone of upright gadroons. Although the sherd is well preserved, it is likely to have been made in a worn or dirty mould and the detail of the decoration is too indistinct for the bowl to be attributable to a particular potter. Flavian. (66).

ii) **Period 2/3?**

Most of the material from the ground surface associated with the later pits was pre-Antonine including:

52.   Form 37, South Gaulish, slightly burnt, showing panel decoration typical of the late Flavian-Trajanic period. The tendril ending in a rosette appears on a bowl from Margidunum in the style of Biragillus (Oswald 1948, pl.XXIV, 1) who also used the Victory (O.814; Knorr 1919, Taf.16, 1). c.A.D.90-110. (62).

53.   (Not illustrated). Form 37, Central Gaulish, showing part
        of a lion devouring a boar (O.1491), probably from a
        freestyle hunting scene. The type was used by potters such
        as Cinnamus and Paternus. Antonine. (50).

iii) **Period** 3. Industrial pits and gullies.

        The fill of pit 46 was mainly Antonine in date. The latest
piece was no. 55 below, dating to the third quarter of the second
century A.D. It included a form 38 with an unidentifiable stamp
ending in]O and:

54.   (Not illustrated). Form 37, Central Gaulish, in the fabric
        of Les Martres-de-Veyre, badly abraded. Beneath the ovolo
        motif, which is indecipherable, is a horizontal row of
        chevrons, possibly that used by Rogers' potter X-12,
        Stanfield's Ioenalis style (S&S, pl.40, 462). c.A.D.
        100-125. (41).

55.   Probably Form 30, Central Gaulish, badly abraded, showing
        panel decoration in the style of Secundus. The ovolo
        (Rogers B.223), Cinnamus' ovolo 1, was used by Secundus
        with a straight border beneath it, as here. The panels show
        a festoon with hare (O.2115) and a vertical impression of
        the dolphin (O.2401) so characteristic of his style. A
        bowl from Leicester (S&S, pl.154, 15) shows all the
        features on the sherd. c.A.D. 150-175. (45).

iii) **Period** 3/4.

        The horizon (6, 43, 47) preceding the later defences
contained a very poorly preserved group of samian ware, of which
the latest was of Hadrianic-Antonine date. It included:

56.   Form 37, South Gaulish, showing panel decoration with a
        figure (not in O.) over straight gadroons beneath two
        panels of leaf-tips and wavy lines, over a basal wreath of
        trifid leaves very common in the Flavian-Trajanic period.
        There is little to suggest a potter, but a bowl signed by
        L.Cosius shows the basal wreath and panels of similar
        leaf-tips (Knorr 1919, Taf.26B). c.A.D.90-110. (43).

57.   Form 37, South Gaulish, showing an ovolo with wavy-line
        border, which is probably that used by the Natalis group of
        Banassac. Trajanic-Hadrianic. (43).

58.   Form 37, Central Gaulish. Two joining sherds of base,
        showing panel decoration with cross motif formed from
        trifid buds; panther (O.1518); festoon over panther
        (O.1570) and uncertain figure. The style is close to that
        of a bowl from London attributed to Acaunissa (S&S, pl.80,

21), which shows the same distinctive rosette at the junctions (presumably Rogers C.28), astragalus across the bead-row and motif made from the same trifid bud. c.A.D. 125-150. (43).

iv) **Periods 4 and 5.** Defences: Phase 2.

The fill of the depression fronting the later rampart (Period 4/5) contained Hadrianic and some Antonine material, including the only complete stamp from the site:

59.(S) Form 27, Central Gaulish, stamped SAC[REM], die 1a of Sacr(i?)e--- of Lezoux [1]. Most of the recorded examples of the stamp are on form 27. It has been noted in the Birdoswald Alley, at Maryport and in an early-Antonine pottery shop at Castleford. The potter's full name is not certain and the faint vertical stroke between the R and E is probably from a scratch on the die rather than a letter. c.A.D. 125-150. (30).

d) **The Playing Fields Car Park, 1973.**

This produced only a small sample of samian, mainly of Flavian or Trajanic date but with a few Hadrianic or early Antonine pieces. A summary of samian found, together with details of three decorated items, will be placed in the site archive.

e) **The Access Road, 1977.**

The samian ware from this site has been listed under the same headings and in the same order as the coarse wares. The decorated ware that is intrinsically interesting or of relevance for dating purposes has been listed in detail, as have all potters stamps.

Although the samian does not provide close dating for the various features on the site, it constitues an interesting collection with a remarkably high proportion of decorated ware. Much of it, however, appears to be residual in context. There is some evidence for disturbance on the site during or after the Roman period, in that sherds from the same bowls occur in several different levels, although generally in the same area of the site. Where sherds are scattered in this way, they have, in the main, been listed under the earliest context in which they appear.

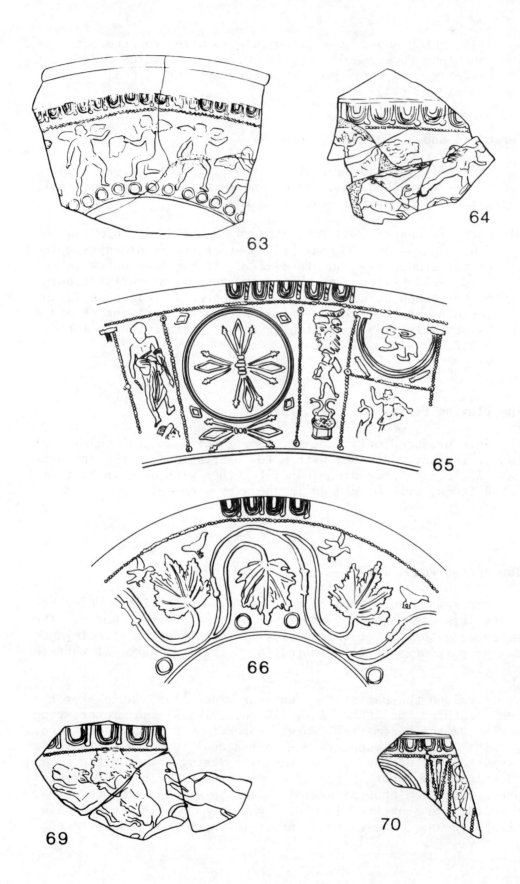

Fig.5. Samian nos. 63-70. Scale 1:2.

The site has produced remarkably little ware of purely Flavian date. Despite the high proportion of decorated ware, only two small sherds of form 29 were present. Two of the stamps (100 & 112) and four decorated bowls (103, 105, 110, 118), two in the style of Germanus, are likely to date before c.A.D.90. It seems unlikely, therefore, that this part of the civil settlement was occupied before the late 80's A.D.

The peak of occupation appears to lie during the Hadrianic-early Antonine period. There is an interesting group of decorated bowls of this date by anonymous and lesser known potters. These include bowls nos, 74, 90 and 129, all of which show a wide basal ridge. Nos. 74 and 129 share characteristics of the potter of Cardurnock (Birley 1947, fig.6, 5, Rogers' potter P.14) who is clearly associated with X.6, as is shown by the ovolo and other characteristics seen on 74 and also on 90. Bowls 120 and 122 show the ovolo later used on his small bowls by Cinnamus, but are clearly the work of earlier potters, 122 showing a wavy line border not used by Cinnamus. Other interesting bowls include 128 in the later style of the Quintilianus group and 63.

Samian ware was reaching the site until the end of the second century A.D., as witnessed by two sherds of form 45 (after c.A.D. 170). However, the later Antonine forms and potters are greatly outnumbered by those of Hadrianic or early Antonine date.

i) **The stone building.**

The samian from this area was broken and scattered, so that in some cases fragments of the same bowl came from several different contexts. In these cases, sherds have been listed under the earliest stratified context.

From below the stone building (section P-Q, 7) with two sherds of South Gaulish ware of Flavian-Trajanic date:

60.   Form 30, Central Gaulish. Seven fragments of a bowl with panel decoration showing a panther (0.1520) over a vertical row of rosettes (Rogers C.55) and leaf tuft (ibid. J.17); Hercules (0.784); the panther (0.1520) over a similar design but with a smaller rosette, possibly Rogers C.29. The ovolo is probably that of Drusus of Lezoux, who used the fine-beaded border, C.55 and both figure types (S&S, pl.88, 1). c.A.D. 125-150. GV S1629-30 (joining GM S1601, 4, 6, 7, 9; feature 11b, 10).

Material from the wall of the stone building (section P-Q, 5) was mostly Central Gaulish and Antonine including:

61.   Form 37, Central Gaulish. Eleven fragments, few joining, showing panel decoration similar to that on a bowl from Lezoux attributed to the style of Laxtucissa (S&S, pl.99, 18). Panels show the dolphin to right (0.2385) over a

warrior (O.193A); triton (O.19) over fleur-de-lys (S&S, fig.27, 2); dolphin to left (O.2394) over warrior (O.193A). The fleur-de-lys appears to have been used by Laxtucissa alone among the associates of Paternus, all of whom used the ovolo and other details. c.A.D. 150-180. DL S873; also FE S1219, (layers 3 & 4); EB S1121 (layer 2); BC S444, 449, 282, DX S993 (top layers of building); AH S142-3, DZ S923 (unstratified).

From layers 3 and 4 of the stone building (section P-Q) among material which was, at the latest, early to mid-Antonine.

62.(S) Form 18/31R, Central Gaulish, stamped LIT.T[ERAF], die 1b of Littera i of Lezoux [1]. There are several examples of this stamp from the Castleford pottery shop of c.A.D. 140-150. It is likely to be one of his later stamps, since one other is in the material from the second London fire. Littera's work is common in the Rhineland, but this particular stamp has only been noted there once. c.A.D. 125-150. FQ S1416.

63. Form 37, Central Gaulish. Three joining fragments, showing a rosette-tongued ovolo with a wavy-line border below and a frieze of alternate Cupids (O.401 and O.504 variant) over a row of rings. The Cupid to the left is considerably smaller than the one illustrated by Oswald. The other exists in a larger size (D.236), also with a missing left hand, as here. The complete version of O.401 appears on bowls by Drusus ii. The implication is that two punches were made, by **surmoulage**, from impressions of D.236, one from the complete figure, the other after the left hand had gone. The style gives no indication of who made the bowl, but the ovolo is of a type current in the Hadrianic and early Antonine periods and the wavy line also suggests a date within this range. c.A.D. 125-145. FE S1231 (also S1232, 4).

64. Form 37, Central Gaulish. Seven joining fragments in the fabric of Les Martres-de-Veyre of a bowl in the style of Cettus, who used the ovolo and acanthus. The decoration is freestyle and shows a lion (uncertain, probably O.1389), Apollo in chariot (O.98) and stag (O.1723). The Apollo and stag were used by Cettus. c.A.D. 135-160. FP S1342 (also FP S1344-6, 1351-3).

65. Form 37, Central Gaulish. Twelve joining fragments of a bowl in the style of Cinnamus, showing his ovolo 3. Decoration shows a double medallion containing the motif made from his triple bud (Rogers G.66); pan mask (O.1214) over gladiator (O.1059) over stand with dolphins; festoon with hare (O.2116) over warrior (probably O.177); draped figure (O.905) over mask (probably O.1339). c.A.D.

150–170. FP S1340 (also FP S1341, 3, 8; FQ S1318–20, GW S1634–6, 1639–42).

66.   Form 37, Central Gaulish. Six fragments of scroll bowl in the style of Cinnamus, showing his ovolo 2 and his birds (O.2239, O.2315). c.A.D. 150–170. FG S1220–2 (joins FE S1225–6; FQ S1320).

From layer 2, stone building (section P–Q) among material mainly of Antonine date:

67.(S)   Form 33, Central Gaulish, stamped DIVICATVS, die 3a of Divicatus of Lezoux [1]. There are numerous examples of this stamp in the burnt material from the Castleford pottery shop of c.A.D.140–150 and it also appears in period IIc at Verulamium which is of the same date. Forms stamped by this potter include 18/31 and 27, but also 80 and Lud Tg. c.A.D. 140–170. EB S1020.

68.(S)   Form 33, Central Gaulish, stamped [MAX]IMI, die 4a of Maximus i of Lezoux [1]. This stamp was only used on cups and has been recorded once on form 27, but otherwise only on form 33. It is in the material from the Verulamium second fire. c.A.D. 150–180.   EB S1243.

69.   Form 37, Central Gaulish. Three joining fragments of freestyle bowl showing a lion devouring a boar (O.1491) and the forepart of a bear (O.1633H). The ovolo is the ovolo 1 of Cinnamus who used both types. c.A.D. 155–175. EB S1118 (joining EB S1120, 1031).

70.   Form 30, Central Gaulish. One fragment showing panel decoration in the style of Divixtus, with his ovolo 4 and caryatid (O.1199). c.A.D. 150–180. EB S1190.

71.   Form 37, Central Gaulish. Four joining fragments showing the ovolo with hammer-headed tongue used by Paternus and his associates, and panels containing a dolphin (O.2384) in a festoon over a leaf (Rogers H.125) and acanthus tips (ibid. K.37), and a medallion with bear (O.1578) and leaf spray (Rogers H.117). The types and details are all attested for Paternus except for the leaf spray, which was used by Quintilianus on his late bowls, close to the style of Laxtucissa (S&S, fig.28, 4; Wild 1975, Fig. 52, 6), but which does not seem to appear on the signed work of the Paternus Group. c.A.D. 160–190. EB S1017; also EB S1024, 1040–1.

72.   Form 37, East Gaulish. Eighteen fragments of bowl showing the stamp IΛ[NVF] of Ianus (or Ianuarius) of Rheinzabern. The upper zone shows festoons containing a basket of fruit (Ricken & Fischer 1963, O.26) and mask (ibid. M.17); the

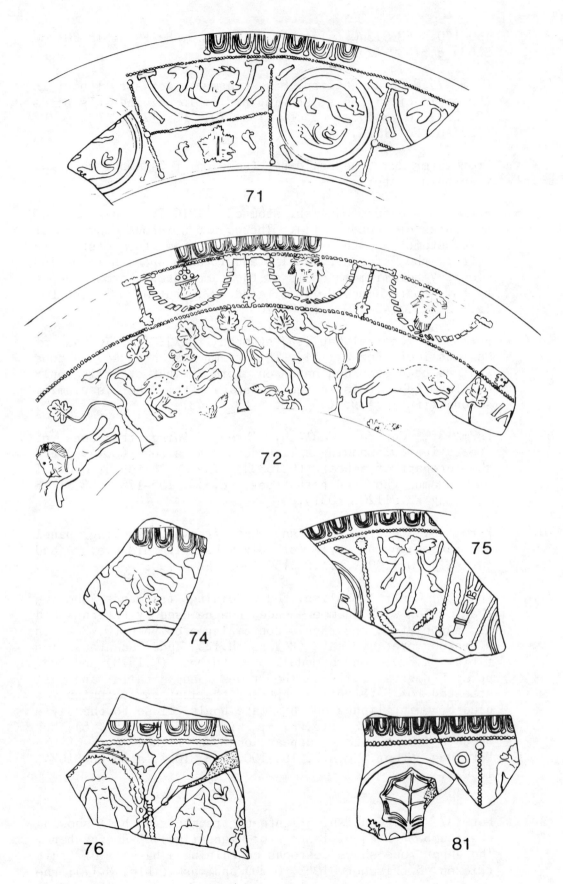

Fig.6.   Samian nos. 71-81.   Scale 1:2.

lower shows a tree motif with a bear (0.1592), horse (0.1906), goat (0.1854) and panther (0.1522). An identical bowl occurs at Rheinzabern (Ricken 1948, Taf.2, 13). The occurrence of work in the style of this potter in the Birdoswald Alley deposit (Richmond & Birley 1930, fig.7, 5) suggests a Hadrianic- early Antonine date. EB S996; also EB S1004-5, 1114, 1129-30, EN S1011, 1016; DX S942, 944-8, CZ S765 (top layers of building); EP S1102, 5 (cobbled area to the North East); AG S132 (unstratified).

From the North West corner of the site (section J-H).

73.(S)   Form 79/80, Central Gaulish, stamped REBVRRIOF, die 41 of Reburrus ii of Lezoux [1]. Reburrus' work includes many examples of both forms 27 and 79. His work seems to have spanned the early to mid- Antonine periods and his stamps occur at Lezoux in a large group of the 150's and in burnt groups from Gauting and the Verulamium second fire. c.A.D. 140-170. (Layer 7; CJ S672).

74.   Form 37, Central Gaulish. The ovolo and wide ridge beneath the decoration were used by X.6 (S&S, pl.75, 13). The decoration is poorly impressed and includes a bear of uncertain type. The eight-petalled rosette and bifid leaf both occur on an anonymous bowl of Hadrianic date from Cardurnock (Birley 1947, fig.6, 5). The basal ridge is another feature of this potter, who shows clear links with X.6 and to whom no.129 below can also be attributed. c.A.D. 125-150. Layer 4; BW S558.

75.   Form 37, Central Gaulish. Five fragments of a panel bowl showing a cupid (0.450) and tripod. The style is probably that of Paternus, who used the cupid, tripod and striated filling ornament (S&S, fig.30, 9, 18). The ovolo is probably a poor impression of his ovolo 1. c.A.D. 160-190. GC S1507-8 (joins with GC S1510, 1513, from layer 6; also CP S882 from the cobbled area to the North East).

76.   Form 37, Central Gaulish. Two joining fragments showing arcade decoration with Pan (0.717) and warrior (0.173A). The style is probably that of Cinnamus or his associates. The ovolo is a slightly smaller version of his ovolo 1. The ovolo, arcade and candelabrum (Rogers Q.27) occur together on a signed bowl (S&S, pl.161, 47). Cinnamus also used the Pan and leaf (Rogers J.93), although the warrior and trifid bud do not appear to be part of his normal repertoire. The ovolo and leaf occur on a bowl showing the rim stamp of Cintusmus (S&S, pl.164, 6), who worked for Cinnamus among other potters. c.A.D. 155-175. Layer 7, CJ S670-1.

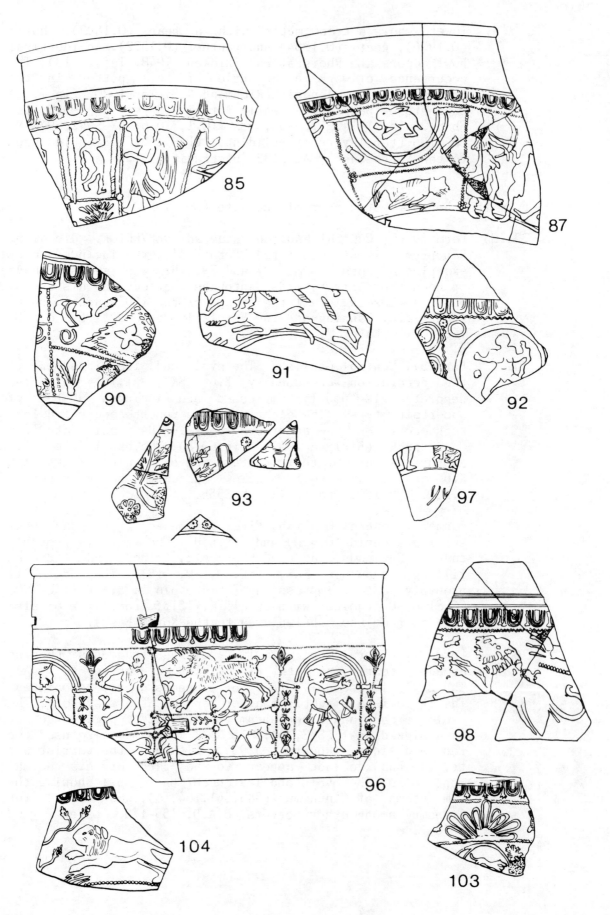

Fig.7.   Samian nos. 85, 87-98, 100-103.   Scale 1:2.

The cobbled area at the North East corner of the site (section F-G, 5) included some later Antonine material, also fragments of bowls 72 and 75 above and:

77.(S) Form 33a, South Gaulish, showing a six petalled rosette stamp, which is also known from Castell Collen. Flavian. GE S1651.

78.(S) Form 27, Central Gaulish, stamped MΛRCELLIVS, die 11a of Marcellus iii of Lezoux [1]. In spite of the reading, the stamp almost certainly belongs to Marcellus iii, to judge by the lettering. It is particularly common on forms 18/31 and 27. Marcellus' work appears in Hadrianic contexts at Lezoux, but he occasionally made forms 79, 79R and 80. This stamp, which occurs at Corbridge and Maryport, is probably to be dated c.A.D. 130-150. GE S1496.

79.(S) Form 33, Central Gaulish, stamped PΛC[Λ TVS ⊦], die 1a of Pacatus ii of Lezoux [3]. Apparently this potter's only stamp, it was used on forms 27, 31 and 33 and appears at sites in the Rhineland, suggesting a date in the first half of the second century. The same die occurs on another cup (no.95 below) of the large kind of form 33 occasionally found in the early Antonine period. Both stamps are clumsily impressed, with thumb-prints across them. c.A.D. 130-150. EO S1085.

80.(S) Form 27, Central Gaulish, stamped [CR]E.IR.O.OFI, die 1a of Criciro v of Lezoux [2]. Criciro's work is relatively common on the Antonine Wall, but rare at sites in the Hadrian's Wall system. This particular stamp appears occasionally on form 27 and on the unusually large version of form 33 which appears to belong to the early Antonine period. c.A.D. 135-160. BZ S567.

81.   Form 37, Central Gaulish. Two joining fragments in the style of Doeccus, who used the ovolo, large-beaded border and leaf. The type is probably the Apollo (0.78) used by him. c.A.D. 160-190. CU S807-8.

From feature 11b (section J-H) came sherds of Hadrianic-Antonine date at the latest. Layer 10 (GM) also included fragments of bowl no.60 above.

82.(S) Form 27, Central Gaulish, stamped SILVI.OF, die 1f of Silvius ii of Lezoux [2]. All the recorded examples of this stamp come from Britain and the Rhineland and it is noticeable that little of his work occurs in France. Most of Silvius' output consists of forms 18/31 and 27. One of his stamps is in a Hadrianic-Antonine pit group at Alcester. c.A.D. 125-145. Layer 9; GK S1579.

83.(S) Form 33/46, South Gaulish, stamped OFFSAB (round a rosette), die 3b of Flavius Sabinus of La Graufesenque [1].

Apart from one stamp at the Saalburg, there is little site dating for this potter. However, his fabrics and frequent use of form 42 and perhaps, occasionally, form Curle 23 suggest a Flavian–Trajanic date. Layer 10; GM S1525.

Road Surfaces.

The earliest material from the early road surfaces was South Gaulish and Flavian or Trajanic. The latest was Hadrianic or early Antonine.

84.(S)   Form 18/31R, Central Gaulish, stamped S‖CVDINVSF, die 6a of Secundinus iii of Lezoux [2]. The dish is a standard form 18/31R of the Hadrianic–Antonine period. The stamp has not been recorded before, but another of this potter's stamps comes from the Saalburg Erdkastell. A decorated bowl from the burnt material in the Castleford pottery shop is almost certainly by him. His forms include many examples of 18/31. c. A.D. 125–145.   FK S1296.

85.   Form 37, South Gaulish. One fragment showing panel decoration with a satyr (0.597) over grass tufts, Victory (0.808B) and part of an animal, probably a stag. The types occur commonly on the bowls from the Bregenz Cellar (Jacobs 1912, 10, 17) and occur on bowls in the style of potters such as Mascuus and Mercato. c.A.D. 90–110.   FK S1297.

86.   Form 37, Central Gaulish. A complete bowl showing the signature of Butrio. The pattern, which does not repeat precisely, shows: mask to right (0.1330) over siren (0.862) over seahorse to left (0.31); Bellerophon and Pegasus (0.835); mask to left (0.1215) over triton (0.25); Apollo in chariot (0.100); cupid (an enlarged version of 0.498) over seahorse to right (0.48); 0.835; cupid with lyre (0.460) over goat (0.1868); 0.100; signature, 0.1215, 0.862, 0.31; 0.835; 0.1330, 0.25, 0.100; 0.1215, 0.48; 0.835; draped figure (0.929) over 0.862; 0.100. The guide line beneath the figures is characteristic of Butrio's work.   c.A.D. 120–145.   FK S1274–8; also EL S1356 (intrusion into early road).

87.   Form 37, Central Gaulish. Seven joining fragments, showing a rivet hole. The panel decoration shows a hare (0.2115) in a festoon over a cock (0.2348), Diana (0.106) and possibly Dionysus (0.571). The ovolo, rosette, borders and all the types were used by potters of the 'Donnaucus-Ioenalis' group of Les Martres-de-Veyre. Work in this style is also found at Lezoux. The fabric of this piece is probably that of Lezoux, suggesting a date c.A.D. 120–130. FT S1370–4 (joins FT S1376).

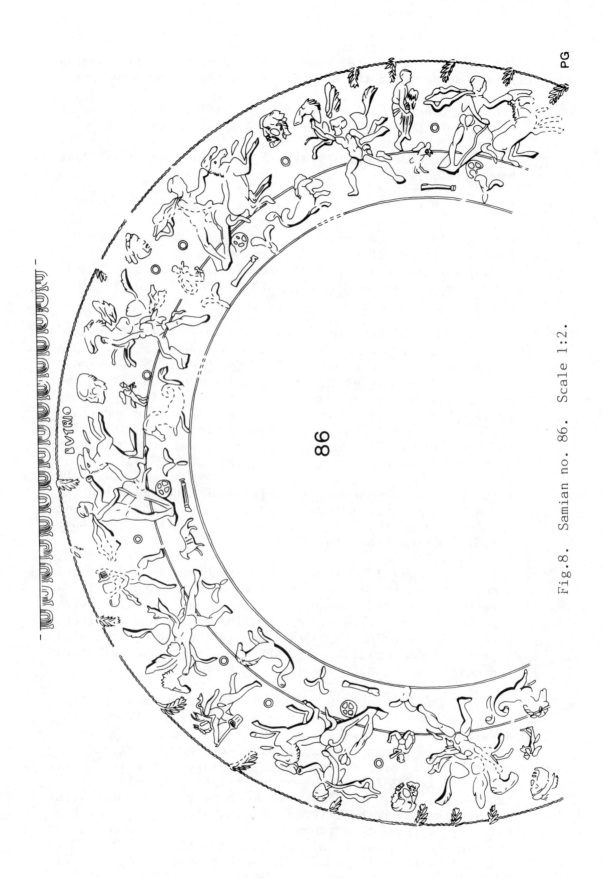

PG

86

Fig.8. Samian no. 86. Scale 1:2.

The layers of the late road produced much residual samian but included some dated to the second half of the second century:

88.(S) Form 33, Central Gaulish, stamped ACV[RIO.FE], die 4a of Acurio of Lezoux [2]. There is no site dating for this stamp, but it was used on forms 18/31, 18/31R, 27 and 38. Acurio also made forms 79 and 80, so his range must have been c.A.D. 145-175.   GH S580.

89.(S) Form 18/31R or 31R, Central Gaulish, stamped RE[GINIOF], die 1a of Reginus iv of Lezoux [2]. There is no close dating evidence for this stamp. It appears once on form 27. The occurrence of Reginus' stamps at sites on Hadrian's Wall and in Antonine Scotland and his usage of form 27 and, more commonly, 79 etc., suggests a date c.A.D. 150-180. BF S528.

90. Form 37, Central Gaulish. The ovolo and basal ridge are similar to those on no.74 above. Both these features are characteristic of the work of X.6, together with the widely spaced bead rows, absence of border to the ovolo and generally untidy scheme of decoration. The pediment (Rogers U.265), leaf cross (ibid. U.9) and trifid bud (S&S, pl.76, 24) all occur on sherds attributed to his style. The pediment and vine scroll (Rogers M.27) were both used by the Quintilianus group. c.A.D. 125-150. BF S526.

91. Form 37, Central Gaulish. One fragment showing a hunting scene in the style of Paternus, with his corded filling ornament, stag (0.1770) and possibly panther (0.1546). c.A.D. 160-190.   AO S254.

92. Form 37, Central Gaulish. One fragment showing panel decoration with coarse wavy-line borders ending in a rosette, a row of concentric circles and medallion with Hercules (0.783 with one snake). The border and rosettes, both at the ends of the border and in the field, were used by Tetturo (S&S, pl.131, 3), who also used a similar ovolo and medallion. c.A.D. 145-170. CH S586.

93. Form 37, Central Gaulish. Seven fragments from a panelled bowl, in the fabric of Les Martres-de-Veyre. Most of the details appear on bowls in the style of Cettus. The ovolo (Rogers B.97) and probably the smaller rosette are on another bowl from Ribchester. The larger rosette (ibid. C.37) and leaf (ibid. H.59) both occur at Les Martres (S&S, pl.143, 36, 46). The figure type, a male scarf-dancer, is not recorded by Dechelette or Oswald, but is on another bowl by Cettus from Rough Castle. There are many other examples of his work in Scotland (Hartley 1972b, 33). c.A.D. 135-160. BF S357 (joins BF S359-60, 436; also BE S349-51, 439 from an intrusion in the late road).

Intrusions in the early road contained sherds from the same

bowls as other layers more closely associated with the early road, including the greater part of the Butrio bowl (no.86) from feature 58. The latest material was probably early Antonine in date and included:

94.(S) Form 27, Central Gaulish, stamped M RCELLIVS, die 11a of Marcellus iii of Lezoux as no.78 above. c.A.D. 130-150. Feature 58. EL S1075.

Early road debris (section G-F, 6) contained material of early Antonine date at the latest. The levels show evidence of considerable disturbance, presumably caused by wear and resurfacing, and sherds from the same bowls occur in levels associated with various road surfaces.

95.(S) Form 33, Central Gaulish, stamped PΛCΛTVS⊦, a largely obliterated impression of die 1a of Pacatus ii of Lezoux [3]. The form is an unusually large cup of form 33 and the die that appearing on no.79 above. c.A.D. 130-150. DY S969.

96. Form 30, Central Gaulish. Three fragments, rivetted together with two lead rivets, showing panel decoration in the style of the 'Donnaucus-Ioenalis' group, with their ovolo and fine-beaded borders. Panels show Pan (O.717) in an arcade; warrior (not in O. or D.) and boar (O.1668) over panthers (smaller versions of O.1518 and O.1566) and deer (O.1763); flute player (O.611) in an arcade. The deer, trifid bud and acanthus were used by Ioenalis (S&S, pl.35, 412) and the small chevron occurs on bowls in a similar style (ibid. 415). The knot (Rogers U.106) was a common feature of the style associated with the Medetus-Ranto group. Bowls in the styles of these Trajanic potters, who started work at Les Martres-de-Veyre, have also been found at Lezoux and the fabric of this bowl suggests an origin at the latter site, probably during the decade A.D. 120-130. DY S940; joins BF S555-6 (late road).

97. Form 37, Central Gaulish, showing part of the cursive signature of Drusus ii of Lezoux beneath the decoration. The types are uncertain, but may possibly be his man (O.570) and the dancer (O.353) which occurs on a bowl signed by him from Watercrook (Wild 1979, fig.120, 72). c.A.D. 125-150. FW S1396.

98. Form 30, Central Gaulish. Three joining fragments showing freestyle decoration with a lion (O.1450), hound (O.1979) and snake-on-rock filling ornament, all used by Attianus and Criciro. The ovolo is Criciro's ovolo 2 (S&S, fig.33, 2). Criciro occasionally used a wavy line border (e.g. S&S, pl.118, 17, which also shows the lion and snake on rock). c.A.D. 135-170. DE S838-40; joins DE S1056.

99. Form 37, Central Gaulish. Many fragments of a hunting

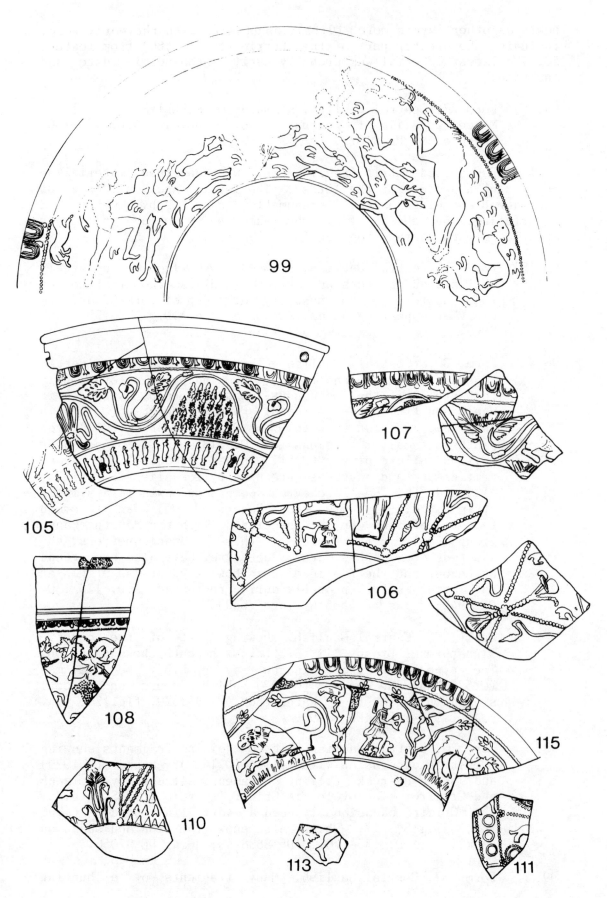

Fig.9. Samian nos. 99, 105–115. Scale 1:2.

scene, with panther (0.1565), bear (0.1617), stag (0.1781), small panther (0.1518), hound (0.1928) and man (0.684A). The ovolo is Cinnamus' ovolo 2. Cinnamus used the panthers and stag, but the other types are not recorded on his signed bowls. The leaf-tip space fillers are a characteristic of his early associates, the Paullus group. c.A.D. 145-170. FW S1388; joins FW S1391-3, EI S1059, DE S885; also BF S575, 7, 530, CH S584-5, 8, 590-1, 720, 722, 728, AO S269 (all from the late road); BE S441 (intrusion in late road); CL S1065 (area between path and road).

Although the area between the path and the road contained some Antonine material, including a fragment of form 37 showing Cinnamus' ovolo 1, c.A.D. 155-175 (CL S691), much of it was South Gaulish and Flavian or Trajanic. There was, once again, evidence that sherds had been widely scattered:

100.(S) Form 27, South Gaulish, stamped OF CELSI, die 1b of Celsus i of La Graufesenque [2]. Celsus' occasional use of forms 24 and Ritterling 9 show that he began work in the Neronian period, but some of his stamps appear at Domitianic foundations. This particular one is known at Binchester and Cannstatt. c.A.D. 75-90. FS S1301.

101.(S) Form 18, South Gaulish, stamped ⟨O⟩F FL⋀GER, die 4b' of Flavius Germanus of La Graufesenque [2]. The original die (4b) continued in use after the breakage of the initial letter and it is in its broken form that it occurs here. There is no evidence of pre-Flavian activity for this potter and many of his stamps appear at Domitianic foundations. This particular one occurs at Okarben. c.A.D. 80-110. CL S710.

102.(S) Form 18/31, South Gaulish, stamped C.IVL.PRM[IC], die 12a of C.Iulius Primic- of La Graufesenque [2]. The die of this stamp must have been broken soon after it was made, since all the other recorded examples lack the initial C. This potter's work is relatively common at Domitianic foundations and there are two examples of the broken die at the Saalburg. c.A.D. 85-110. EZ S1235.

103. Form 37, South Gaulish. Two fragments of bowl with zonal decoration in the style of Germanus, who used the tree, lion (0.1453) and rock ornament (Knorr 1952, Taf.28E). c.A.D. 75-90. DU S1047, 9.

104. Form 37, South Gaulish. One fragment of bowl with zonal decoration, showing the ovolo with four-pronged terminal used by M.Crestio and Crucuro. The small hound (0.1931) was used by both potters and the leaf is probably that of M.Crestio (Knorr 1919, Taf.28, 26). c.A.D. 80-100. CL S889.

105.	Form 37, South Gaulish. Four joining fragments, three unstratified, the other slightly burnt. The bowl shows the remains of three lead rivets and two further rivet holes. The decoration shows a leaf scroll. The ovolo occurs on a bowl from La Graufesenque (Hermet 1934, pl.82, 7) stamped C.I.SA, a stamp which also occurs on a bowl stamped inside by Pudens (ibid. pl.114, 15 & 15a). A similar scroll with the ivy leaf appears on a form 29 by Iucundus (Knorr 1952, Taf.31E) and the larger leaf on an unpublished Neronian-early Flavian form 29 from Gloucester. The form and ovolo suggest a date c.A.D. 75-100. DM S860; also BQ S518-20.

106.	Form 37, South Gaulish. Three fragments, two joining, of a bowl with panel decoration showing a saltire with Nile goose (0.2244), altar (Hermet 1934, pl.16, 69) over Mercury with a goat (smaller version of 0.548) and part of an uncertain, draped type, deeply impressed. Parallels to the saltire motif are common at Bregenz. The closest parallel (Jacobs 1912, 27) shows the same bud and bead row beneath the type. The bud was used by L.Cosius, Severus and the potter stamping OFFEIC, all predominantly Flavian potters. The general style, however, is more typical of Flavian-Trajanic products. c.A.D. 80-110. FS S1302; also DU S1050; AB S51 (unstratified).

107.	Form 37, South Gaulish. Four fragments of bowl showing a leaf scroll with a stag (0.1699). The leaf, although earlier used by Flavian potters such as Biragillus, Patricius and Fl.Germanus (Knorr 1919, Textb.12), also occurs on a bowl from Ovilava in the style of Mercato (Karnitsch 1959, Taf.14, 1). This is probably the closest parallel to the bowl. The grass motif and stag were also used by Mercato and the scroll binding, though blurred, may well be his. c.A.D. 90-110. CL S640, BO S559; also AP S158-9 (late road).

108.	Form 30, Central Gaulish. Two joining fragments in the style of the 'Donnaucus-Ioenalis' group of Les Martres-de-Veyre, showing their small-beaded border, vine scroll and bird (0.2315A); cf. S&S, pl.49, 577. c.A.D. 100-125. BT S550; also BT S810.

From the pit, feature 60, came Antonine material including a fragment of bowl with Cinnamus' ovolo 2, another decorated sherd probably also in his style (c.A.D. 150-170) and:

109.(S)	Form 33, Central Gaulish, stamped VAGIR[OF], die 4a of Vagiro or Vagirus of Lezoux [2]. The dating of this potter rests entirely on his forms, which include 18/31, 18/31R or 31R, 27, 31 and 80. He seems to have used both forms of his name indiscriminately and some of his stamps are ungrammatical. c.A.D. 145-175. EY S1664.

The latest material from the path was Hadrianic or early Antonine:

110.   Form 37, South Gaulish. One fragment showing zonal decoration with a running stag and panel of wavy lines and leaf tips. The plant motif occurs on a sherd of form 29 from Gunzberg (Knorr 1919, Textb.45c) and on the Hartlip flagon, signed by Sabinus (O&P, pl.85, 2). The flagon also shows leaftip decoration, similarly spaced. c.A.D. 75-90. DP S1051.

111.   Form 37, Central Gaulish. One fragment showing panel decoration. Insufficient survives for a precise identification of the types, but the beaded ring and festoon are similar to those used by the Hadrianic-Antonine potters such as Secundinus, Arcanus and Drusus, suggesting a date c.A.D. 125-150. DP S1052.

The contents of the drainage channel were mainly South Gaulish and Flavian or Trajanic, but the latest pieces were in Lezoux fabric and Hadrianic or early Antonine:

From Section C-D, 8:
112.(S) Form 27, South Gaulish, stamped [OF] COELI, die 1a of Coelus of La Graufesenque [1]. The record for this stamp seems to be entirely Flavian. It includes sites founded under Domitian (Butzbach, Corbridge and the Saalburg) and many bowls of form 29. c.A.D. 70-90. CW S788.

113.   Form 37, Central Gaulish. Small scrap showing vine leaf and part of a figure. The vine scroll was used by the 'Donnaucus-Ioenalis' group (S&S, pl.46, 545). The fabric is probably that of Lezoux, suggesting a Hadrianic date. CW S791.

From Section C-D ,56:
114.   (Not illustrated). Form 29, South Gaulish. One fragment showing an upper zone with scroll and a lower zone, worn, but possibly showing straight gadroons. Probably early Flavian. CN S759.

115.   Form 37, South Gaulish. Many fragments from a rather poorly-produced bowl. The decoration shows a lion (0.1419), Diana (0.110) and stag (0.1709), divided by trees surmounted by birds (0.2248, 0.2293). The general style and types are typical of the late Flavian-Trajanic period. Similar trees and grass tufts occur on a bowl from the Bregenz Cellar deposit in a style similar to Mascuus and his associates (Jacobs 1912, 4). c.A.D. 90-110. CN S753-5; also CN S758; FL S1257, 1253 (from Section A-B, 9, C-D, 2 as nos. 117-120 below).

116.   Form 37, Central Gaulish. The decoration shows a freestyle hunting scene with panther (0.1570), leaf and panther

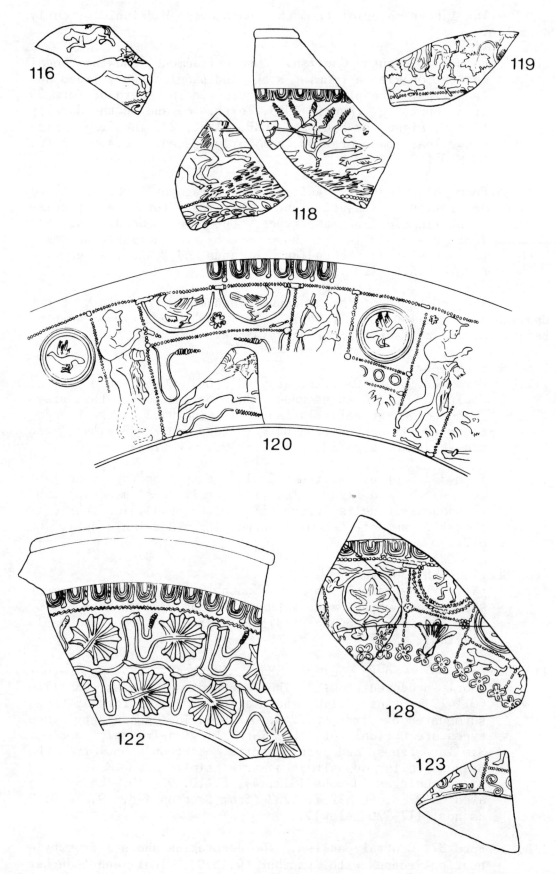

Fig.10. Samian nos. 116–128. Scale 1:2.

(probably O.1542). Beneath the decoration is a basal wreath of rams' horns, bordered by a wavy line. The general style is that of the Trajanic–Hadrianic potters of Les Martres-de-Veyre, several of whom used a similar wreath. CN S751.

The group also produced a small fragment probably from bowl no.123 below.

Section A–B, 9 & section C–D, 2:
117.(S) Form 18/31, Central Gaulish, stamped PATERN[VS. Γ], die 3a of Paternus iii of Lezoux [2]. This is the stamp of the Lezoux Paternus who was associated with Ianuarius ii in the production of decorated ware. His work is common in the Rhineland and one of his stamps is in the material from the Castleford pottery shop of c.A.D. 140–150. This particular stamp occurs on forms 18/31R, 27 and 81. c.A.D. 135–155. BI S1464.

118.   Form 37, South Gaulish. Four fragments showing a horseman (O.255) spearing a boar (slightly larger than O.1670). The ovolo and horseman were used by Germanus. A bowl in his style from the Bregenz Cellar deposit (Jacobs 1912, 3) shows the ovolo, tree, boar, rock motif and a similar basal wreath. c.A.D. 75–90. BI S508; also BI S510, 11; CL S811 (between the path and the road).

119.   Form 30, Central Gaulish, showing a vine-scroll decoration in the style of the 'Donnaucus-Ioenalis' group, with cupid (O.408), possibly the dancer O.354 and a horse (not in O., but common on pieces in this style, e.g. S&S, pl.42, 487). The fabric is probably that of Lezoux rather than Les Martres-de-Veyre, suggesting a date probably c.A.D. 120–125. BI S393.

120.   Form 37, Central Gaulish. Many fragments of a bowl with panel decoration showing Diana (O.107); bird (O.2317) in a medallion over a boar (O.1666); man (O.638, slightly larger version); birds (O.2295A, O.2250A) in festoons probably over a panel with a horse (O.1894); O.107; bird (O.2326) in a medallion, etc. The ovolo is Cinnamus' ovolo 2. However, not all the figure types are part of Cinnamus' normal repertoire and the bowl is more likely to be connected with his earlier associates. The striated tendril occurs on a bowl in Sacer-Attianus style from Wanborough. The leaf-tip space filler was a characteristic feature of Attianus, who also used the boar, horse and birds (O.2250A, O.2295A). The figure types suggest a connection with Austrus, who used O.107, O.638, and the birds O.2317 and O.2326, (S&S, pl.95, 20 and 23). The rosette also appears to be closer to his (ibid. 20) than to that of Sacer and Cinnamus. Although Cinnamus himself is unlikely to have used the ovolo much before A.D. 150, a Hadrianic-Antonine date seems likely for this piece. c.A.D. 130–160. BI S387-8; also BI S392, 397-8, 400,

474-7, 482, 484, 490-1, 507, 509; AF S140, AN S203 (above drainage channel).

Although levels above the drainage channel (section E-A, 3 & 4) contained some purely Antonine material dating from early in the second half of the second century, most of the samian was earlier, including two sherds from bowl no.120 above.

121.(S) Form 33, Central Gaulish, stamped REGALIS.F, die 4a of Regalis i of Lezoux [2]. This stamp occurs at Benwell and was used on forms 18/31R, 31R and 79R. Others occur on 27 (occasionally), 80 and Lud.Tg. c.A.D. 150-180. AN S242.

122.   Form 37, Central Gaulish. Six fragments of bowl showing leaf scroll decoration. The ovolo is the same as on no 120 above, Cinnamus' ovolo 2, though Cinnamus himself did not use the wavy line border. The ovolo and leaf occur together on a bowl from the Birdoswald Alley (Richmond & Birley 1930, fig.4) and also on one at Slack. The style and site evidence suggest a Hadrianic date, c.A.D. 125-140. CE S658; also CE S660, BD S405, 408; BI S466 (drainage channel as 117-120 above); BC S864 (top layers of building).

123.   Form 37, Central Gaulish. One fragment showing the characteristic S-motif of the Large S potter. The man may be 0.570, which occurs on fragments in the similar style of X.6 (S&S, pl.76, 27). c.A.D. 125-150. CE S657.

Unstratified

124.(S) Form 31, Central Gaulish, stamped CER[IALI.MA], die 2a of Cerialis ii of Lezoux [1]. This stamp appears most frequently on forms 18/31, 18/31R and 27. The site evidence includes the Castleford pottery shop of the 140's, Hadrian's Wall (Chesters Museum), Hardknott and Newstead. c.A.D. 140-165. GQ S1535.

125.(S) Form 33, Central Gaulish, stamped [MI]CCI.VSF, die 1a of Miccius of Lezoux [1]. This stamp was frequently used on form 18/31R and occurs once on form 79. There is one example from Chesterholm. c.A.D. 140-165. AB S50.

126.(S) Form 27, Central Gaulish, stamped SILVI.OF, die 1h of Silvius ii of Lezoux [1]. For the dating evidence see no.82 above. c.A.D. 125-145. BQ S518.

127.(S) Form 18/31, Central Gaulish. Die 5b of Viducus ii of Les Martres-de-Veyre [2]. There is no dating evidence for this stamp, but another by this potter is in material from the London Second Fire and there is one example from Malton. c.A.D. 105-125. BA S427-8.

128.   Form 37, Central Gaulish. Five fragments of bowl with
        panel decoration showing a vine-scroll with birds (O.2262B,
        O.2294); cupid (O.422) in a festoon over a bud motif;
        festoon over panther or reptile (O.1554). The style is
        that of Quintilianus, who used the ovolo, basal wreath of
        rosettes (S&S, pl.68, 1) and O.1554. The ovolo, beaded
        borders and rosette wreath are features of his later style
        and the date is likely to be towards the end of the period
        c.A.D. 125-150. AB S52; also AB S57, 60, 74, 77.

129.   Form 37, Central Gaulish. Three joining fragments of bowl
        showing panel decoration with a Victory (a smaller version
        of O.826) and Apollo (O.83). The style is that of an
        anonymous Hadrianic potter related to X.6, who used the
        large rosette (Rogers P.14) and high basal ridge and whose
        work is known from Cardurnock (Birley 1947, Fig.6, 5) and
        other sites in the Hadrian's Wall area. Both features also
        occur on no.74 above. c.A.D. 125-150. AB S1; also AB S18,
        25.

f) **The School Field, 1974.**

        A summary of all groups will be placed in the site archive.
Only stamps and relevant decorated sherds have been described
below.

Trench C, pit, with Antonine material which is clearly residual:

130.(S) 'Patera' handle, Central Gaulish, with a mould stamp in the
        decoration reading D.OCC.I.VSF (ret.). The die is 4b of
        Doccius ii of Lezoux [2]. This is the second of Doccius'
        stamps to have been recorded on a patera handle (cf.
        Dechelette 1904, ii, p.318, from a different die). The
        stamp in question here is only otherwise known on forms 37
        (in a highly individual style) and 79R. Doccius' record
        includes one example of form 27, but his other forms and
        his decorative style place him in the mid- to late-Antonine
        period. One of his stamps comes from the Brougham
        cemetery. c.A.D. 155-180. C6.

131.   Form 37, East Gaulish. The ovolo appears to be Ricken's
        ovolo C from La Madeleine (Ricken 1934, taf.7), which with
        the beaded border has been noted on bowls from Antonine
        sites in Scotland, including Birrens (Wild 1975, fig.59,
        94). The Minerva (O.126A) and rosette, however, have
        apparently not been noted from La Madeleine. c.A.D.
        130-160. C8.

Trench A. Pre-Masonry building with other material none of which need be later than the Hadrianic period:

132.(S) Form 27, Central Gaulish. Three fragments, one stamped [BUR]RIUS.[F..], part of an incomplete stamp of Burrius (die incomplete 1). The fabric of this and one of the other two recorded examples of this stamp suggests manufacture at Les Martres-de-Veyre. The unusual style of the V's adds further weight to the argument, cf. Agedillus ii and Iulius Talussa (Terrise 1968, pl.52, 54). c.A.D. 100–125. A6.

133. Form 37, South Gaulish. One fragment showing scroll decoration. The pointed leaf was used by several of the Flavian potters, as was the leaf-tip panel. The scroll and general style of decoration appears on two bowls in the style of M.Crestio from Margidunum (Oswald 1948, pl.22, 6, 8) and also on bowl no.107 above. The form and general style suggest a date c.A.D. 80–100. A6.

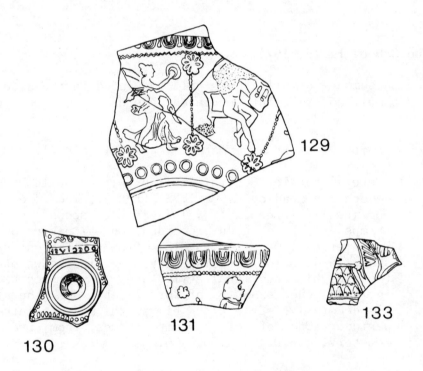

Fig.11. Samian nos. 129–133. Scale 1:2.

g) **The Primary School foundations, 1977.**

The samian from the school foundation trenches was mostly Flavian or Flavian-Trajanic in date, although it included about 28% of wares of later date (down to the later Antonine period). Only the stamps and significant decorated ware are listed below.

134.(S) Form 18, South Gaulish, stamped OFC[.EN], die 3b of Censori of La Graufesenque [2]. The record for this stamp seems to be entirely Flavian and includes sites such as Caerleon, Catterick, Corbridge and the York fortress. c.A.D.70-100. SZ S114.

135.(S) Form 33, Central Gaulish, stamped [IVS]TINA, die 2b of Iustus ii of Lezoux [1]. This stamp is known from Chesterholm and the Pudding Pan Rock wreck. This, together with the evidence of his decorated ware, suggests a date c.A.D. 160-190 for this potter. ZT S16.

136. Form 29, South Gaulish. An almost complete bowl, stamped MEOILLVS, die 5a of Meddillus of La Graufesenque [1]. The details of the bowl are not ones normally associated with this stamp. The feathery leaf in the scroll in the upper zone is on a bowl from London stamped by the Bassus i -Coelus association (Knorr 1952, Taf.10E) and on an unstamped piece from Fishbourne (Period 1B-C; Dannell 1971, fig.127, 11). The basal wreath is on a bowl from Risstissen stamped by Seno (Knorr 1919, Taf.78B), which has decoration similar to the Ribchester piece. This stamp of Meddillus is nearly always on form 29, many with decoration typical of the Vespasianic period, but some in pre-Flavian style. One example appears at Verulamium in Period I (c.A.D. 49-60), but there are others from Caerleon, Cardiff and York. c.A.D. 60-85. ZQ S115.

137. Form 29, South Gaulish. Fragment of upper zone showing a panel with poppy-head motif, birds (0.2247, 0.2290) and Nile geese (0.2244, 0.2286). The poppy-head and all the birds are very common on bowls of the Neronian- early Flavian period. The poppy-head occurs on bowls by Mommo from the Pompeii Hoard (Atkinson 1914, 9-11) although always as part of a saltire rather than separately, as here. c.A.D. 65-85. ZS S21.

138. Form 30, South Gaulish, in the style of Germanus, showing his tree, rock motif and stags (0.1700, 1746). All these features occur together on a signed bowl from Rottweil (Knorr 1952, Taf. 28E). c.A.D. 60-85. ZP S69.

139. Form 37, South Gaulish. Two joining fragments of zonal bowl, showing the four-pronged ovolo of M.Crestio and Crucuro, their S-shaped gadroons and the hound (0.1927) used by M.Crestio (Knorr 1919, Textb.17E). c.A.D. 80-100. ZV S34.

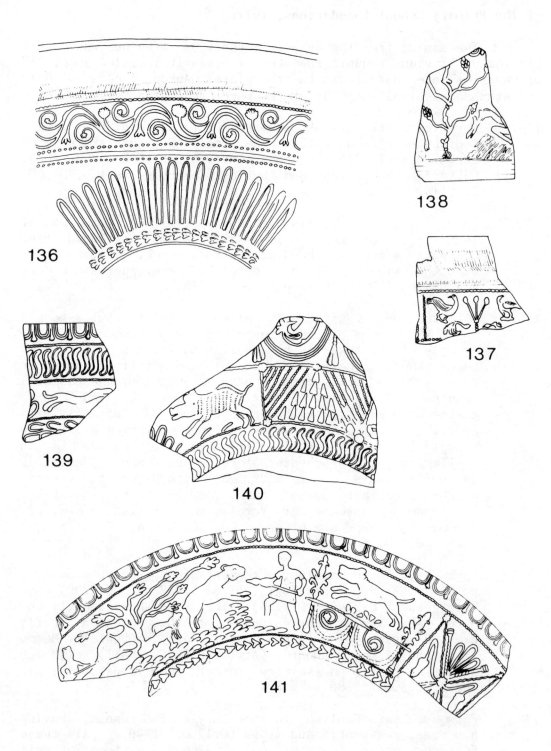

Fig.12. Samian nos. 136-141. Scale 1:2.

140.   Form 37, South Gaulish, showing zonal decoration typical of
        the Domitianic period. The boar (O.1670) was used by
        Crucuro, Rufinus and Secundus, the gadroons (see 139 above)
        by M.Crestio and Crucuro. A bowl from Brecon, attributed
        by Pryce to the style of Severus, shows the boar, bush and
        grass blade (Wheeler 1926, S148). A stamped bowl by
        Severus from Nettleton Scrubb shows the stirrup leaf,
        festoon and possibly the pendant. c.A.D. 80-100. ZO S97.

141.   Form 37, South Gaulish. Eight joining fragments of bowl
        showing saltire and wide panel containing a hunting scene.
        The types are the hunter in a chariot (probably a larger
        form of the Diana O.118), goats (O.1860), bear (?),
        huntsman (O.1102) and hound (O.1994) over a short length of
        festoon decoration. The festoons and basal wreath were
        used by Vitalis (Knorr 1919, Taf.84F, G). They occur
        together as here, adjoining a saltire, on an unpublished
        bowl from Gloucester, which also shows the same triple leaf
        bud motif which occurs in the saltire here. A similar
        saltire was used on a bowl from Margidunum (Oswald 1948,
        pl.25, 20) in the style of Mercato, on bowls in whose style
        most of the figure types appear. c.A.D. 90-110. ZS S1.

142.   Form 30, South Gaulish. Several sherds of a bowl with
        panel decoration showing: a) saltire; b) warrior (O.164A);
        c) hare (O.2129) over bird (O.2266); d) figure uncertain;
        e) hound (O.2004) over bird (O.2231); arranged a-b-c-d-a-b-
        e-d, repeated twice round the bowl. The style is that of
        the Flavian-Trajanic potters of La Graufesenque. The
        animal and bird types occur on bowls in the style of
        Mercato and on a bowl in the Bregenz Cellar deposit in
        Mascuus' style. The motifs in the saltire were all used by
        Mercato (Knorr 1919, Taf.57A, D). c.A.D. 90-110. ZQ S44.

143.   Form 37, South Gaulish. Two joining fragments showing
        clumsy, ill-defined panel decoration of the type associated
        with the latest products of La Graufesenque. The types are
        a smaller version of the Bacchus, O.586; a fragmentary
        type, uncertain; a smaller version of the Venus, O.313,
        which occurs on a bowl from the Bregenz Cellar (Jacobs
        1912, 21); and a satyr (O.630), attributed to the style of
        L.Cosius (Knorr 1919, Taf.25, 7). c.A.D. 90-110. ZP S94.

144.   Form 37, Central Gaulish, showing the ovolo and thick-roped
        borders of Iullinus (cf. S&S, pl.127, 30, in his style) and
        the woman at altar (O.322) which also appears in work in
        his style. c.A.D. 160-190. ZQ S54.

145.   Form 30, East Gaulish, showing a warrior and female figure
        (Ricken & Fischer 1963, M.177, M.246). Both types were used
        by Cobnertus III and Comitialis V of Rheinzabern. They
        occur together on a bowl by Comitialis (Ricken 1948,
        taf.96, 17) which shows the same juxtaposition of
        incongruous types. On the whole, the piece is more likely

to belong to the earlier potter Cobnertus, as form 30 is rare in the third century A.D. and an Antonine date seems more probable. ZW S7.

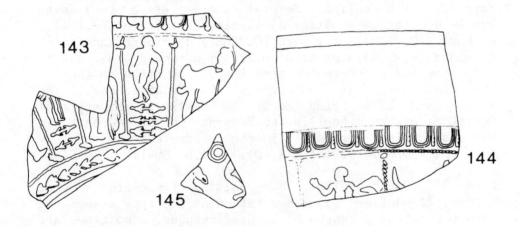

Fig.13. Samian nos. 142-144. Scale 1:2.

Chapter 2.
COARSE POTTERY

By R.C.Turner, P.V.Webster & J.H.S.Witherington.
With contributions by P.Gibbons, K.F.Hartley, L.Hird & J.J.Patterson.

In this chapter we have gathered together coarse pottery reports which were originally written separately to accompany the structural reports in Part 2. The major author of each report is indicated in its title. Other contributors are indicated either at the beginning of relevant sub-sections or in the form of initials after individual entries.

The pottery from recent fort excavations has already been the subject of general comment (Edwards & Webster 1985, 59-61) and it is our intention to make an overall summary of coarse pottery evidence in a later volume in this series. However, as this volume includes details of most of the coarse pottery recovered from the civil settlement in recent years, some brief comment seems called for.

The overall picture provided by the pottery published below supports the view of a civil settlement intensely occupied in the later first and second centuries. Thereafter, occupation appears to have been on a reduced scale and restricted to small areas. Only Anchor Hill (section b below) contains much fourth century pottery and only the School Field and area (section g) much which is certainly third century. Unless the pattern is radically different in those parts of the vicus not yet sampled, or already removed by river action (and it has to be said that this is not impossible) it would seem that the early third century occupation was concentrated near the East Gate of the fort where a major building appears to have stood in the third century. However, the late Anchor Hill material, the late date of the defences (section d) and a scatter of late pottery elsewhere suggest that settlement pattern in the northern vicus is, as yet, incomplete. to yield all

Although late fourth century pottery is fairly well represented in the fort (cf. Edwards & Webster 1985, Fig.19, passim; also material in the Ribchester Museum to be surveyed in a later volume in this series) very little of this distinctive pottery finds its way onto the civil settlement sites reported here. It may also be noted that the pattern is the same on the only two major sites not reported upon here. The Water Street site was predominantly first and second century. The Bath-house appears to have ceased to function by the mid third century (cf. LAB, 5, no.6 [1980] pp.14-15). The apparent lack of occupation in the civil settlement during the late fourth century may well have implications for the character of the latest occupation inside the fort, a matter further discussed in the introduction to Part 2.

A brief summary of the sources of pottery reaching Roman Ribchester has already been given in relation to the fort pottery

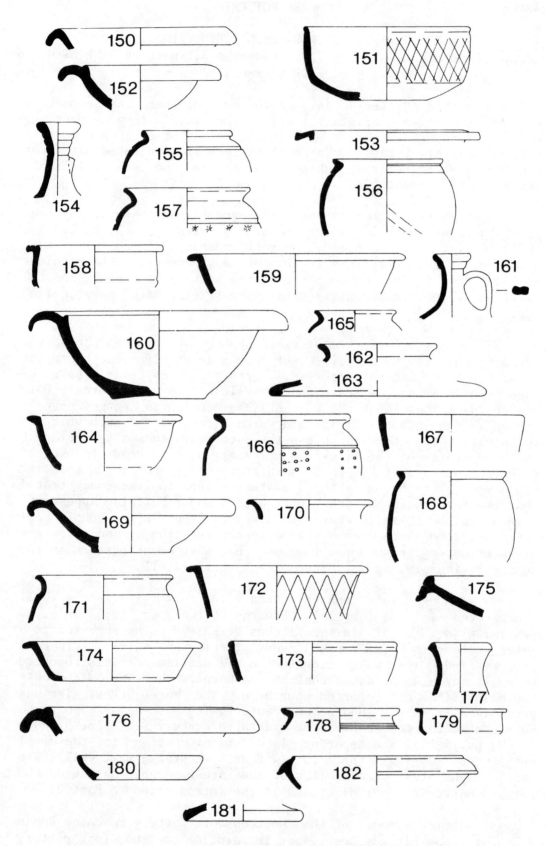

Fig.14. Coarse pottery nos. 150–182. Scale 1:4.

(Edwards & Webster 1985, Chapter 6). As one would expect, the sources of vicus pottery are virtually identical and need occasion no further comment here. Differences in the pattern between individual sites do, of course, occur (see, for instance, the larger sample of colour coated wares from the School Field site) but these are discussed, where relevant, in individual sub-sections below.

a) **The Playing Fields, 1968–9.**
   By P.V.Webster.

There was no significant pottery from Phase 1.

i) **Phase 2.**

From levelling prior to building:
150.   Bowl in a fabric which is now burnt grey but was possibly originally fawn. Perhaps from a vessel similar to Gillam 1970, type 291 (A.D. 80–120).   1.8.

151.   Bowl in Black-burnished ware; cf. Gillam 1976, no.52 (mid to late 2nd century).   1.8.

152.   Mortarium in light red fabric with a thin white slip and white grits. This mortarium could well have been made at Wilderspool (KFH).   1.8b.

From a wattle wall in Building 3:
153.   Flanged bowl in pink mica-dusted fabric; cf. Newstead (Curle 1911) fig.26, 13 (c.A.D.80–105).   1.102.

From the floor of Building 3:
154.   Ring-neck flagon in light red fabric with traces of a white slip.   See no.161 below for a discussion of the type. Perhaps late 1st to mid 2nd century.   1.101.

155.   Jar in grey fabric; cf. Gillam 1970, no.96 (A.D.80–120). 1.101.

156.   Jar in black fabric with a single line of smoothed decoration diagonally on the surviving fragment; cf. Turret 48b (Shaw 1926) no.7 (c.A.D.122–140).   1.101.

157.   Jar in black fabric with rusticated decoration. Rusticated ware does not seem to have been in production in the north after the very early 2nd century (cf. Thompson 1958, pp.15–51).   Late 1st to early 2nd century.   1.101.

From Pit 2.16a:

158.   Flanged bowl with a reeded rim in a light grey fabric. One
         of the common Flavian-Trajanic flanged and carinated bowl
         series (cf. Gillam 1970, types 214-5).   2.16a.

159.   Flanged dish in Black-burnished ware.   The exterior shows
         vertical burnishing. For the general form see Gillam 1976,
         nos. 54 & 56 (early to mid 2nd century).   2.16a.

160.   Mortarium in light red fabric with a white slip and white
         grits (cf. no.152 above).   2.16a.

From levelling over pit 2.16a:

161.   Small ring-necked flagon of a similar type to Gillam 1970,
         type 5 (c.A.D. 110-150).   Gillam dates his type 5 later
         than the flagons with angular rings (his types 1-4).
         However, the latter do not seem to have been marketted in
         the southern Pennines. Slack, for instance, produces only
         flagons of Gillam type 5 (or later types), cf. Dodd &
         Woodward 1922, nos. 115-8. It may well be, therefore, that
         flagons of type 5 have a longer currency south of the Wall
         zone and a late 1st to mid 2nd century date for the type is
         suggested here. 2.16.

162.   Jar in hard dark grey ware; cf. Chesterholm (Birley 1938)
         no.44 (c.A.D.79-125) and Old Kilpatrick (Miller 1928)
         pl.xxi, 2. Late 1st to mid 2nd century.   2.16.

163.   Lid in light grey smooth fabric.   2.16.

Levelling prior to phase 3:

164.   Flanged bowl in grey burnished   fabric.   This vessel
         resembles Black-burnished ware bowls of Hadrianic-Antonine
         date.   2.14.

Contemporary with phase 2:

165.   Jar in dark grey fabric; similar to Black-burnished ware
         vessels such as Gillam 1970, type 122 (early to mid 2nd
         century) and presumably of a similar date.   3.3.

ii) **Phase 3.**

From a road surface:

166.   Jar in hard mid grey fabric decorated in applied dots in
         the same fabric. The decoration occurs in Flavian-Trajanic
         contexts (cf. Gillam 1970, type 68, c.A.D. 80-130) as well
         as in later contexts (see, for instance, the poppy head
         beakers, ibid. types 70-1, c.A.D. 120-200).   The general
         shape of our vessel suggests a Flavian-Trajanic date, cf.

Corbridge (Forster & Knowles 1912) no.26, c.A.D. 79-125.
1.43.

167.   Dish in smooth grey fabric. 1.43.

From the destruction of Building 10 or the levelling for Building 11:
168.   Beaker in light red sandy fabric; possibly a Wilderspool
        product. 2.8.

169.   Mortarium in light red fabric with traces of white slip;
        cf. no.152 above. 2.8.

Probably associated with Building 13:
170:    Jar in smoothed black fabric. It is perhaps intended to be
        reminiscent of Hadrianic-Antonine jars in Black-burnished
        ware. 2.64.

Resting on the stone surface of 2.67, associated with Building 13:
171.   Jar in mid-grey fabric; cf. Chesterholm (Birley 1938) no.22
        (c.A.D. 79-122). 2.114.

172.   Flanged bowl in Black-burnished ware; cf. Gillam 1976,
        no.34 (early to mid 2nd century). 2.114.

173.   Bowl in Black-burnished ware; cf. Gillam 1976, no.68 (early
        to mid 2nd century). 2.114.

Lower fill of pit 2.62:
174.   Flanged dish in Black-burnished ware; cf. Gillam 1976,
        no.63 (mid to late 2nd century). 2.61.

iii) **Phase 4**:

From the phase 4 stone dump:
175.   Hammer-head mortarium in white fabric from the Mancetter
        -Hartshill potteries. Probably c.A.D. 180-240. (KFH).
        3.8.

176.   Mortarium in white fabric from the Mancetter-Hartshill
        potteries. c.A.D. 150-190. (KFH) 3.8.

iv) **Unstratified**.

The unstratified pottery nearly all fell within the date
range c.A.D.80-200. The following are of interest as they are not
represented above:

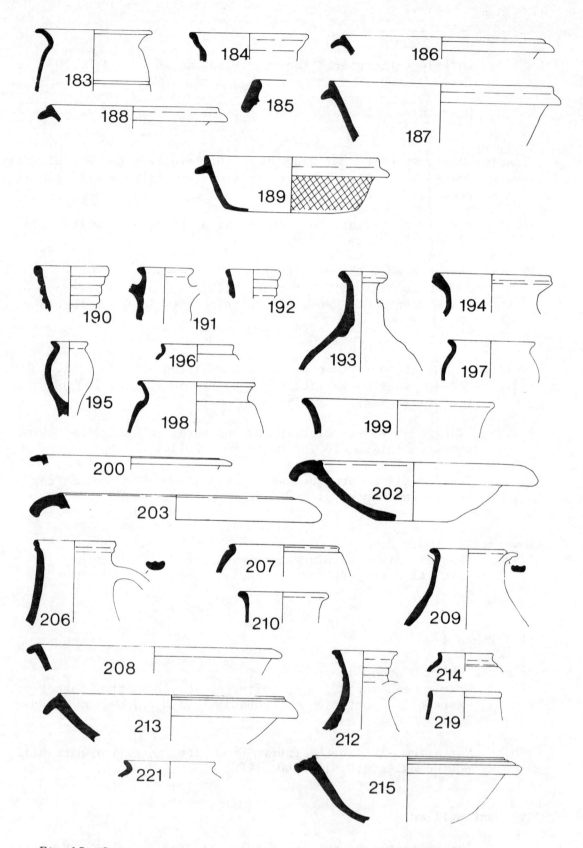

Fig.15. Coarse pottery nos. 183-215, 219 & 221.   Scale 1:4.

177.   Flagon in light red fabric; cf. Gillam 1970, type 11 (c.A.D. 80-100).

178.   Jar in light red fabric.

179.   Flanged bowl in light red fabric; a very small example of the common Flavian-Trajanic flanged and carinated bowl.

180.   Small dish or possibly a lid in light red fabric.

181.   Lid in grey fabric.

182.   Mortar-like bowl in dark pink fabric. It resembles the mortarium, Gillam 1970, type 273 (c.A.D. 240-300) and is thus the only piece recovered that may be later than c.A.D. 200.

b) **Anchor Hill**
by P.V.Webster.

The site at Anchor Hill was the subject of small scale excavation by John Dewhurst and the Ribble Archaeological Society in 1967. The area produced a wide range of samian and coarse pottery indicating activity from the late first/ early second century through to the mid fourth century. Both samian and coarse pottery were reported upon soon after the excavation was completed and reports upon both with unreduced drawings of the coarse pottery will be found in the Ribchester archive at the Lancashire Record Office, Preston. The earlier pottery requires little comment, although it does confirm the spread of the first to second century civil settlement to the north-west of the fort. The later pottery is, however, of greater interest because so little third and fourth century pottery has so far been found in the civil settlement. As the later pottery from Anchor Hill is refered to several times in our discussions of the Civil Settlement, we have taken the opportunity to publish here the more diagnostic later pieces.

183.   Jar in Black-burnished ware; cf. Gillam 1976, no.10 (late 3rd century). AN (excavation code). IX (archive number).

184.   Jar in Black-burnished ware. The flaring character of the rim is typical of late jars (cf. Gillam 1976, no.14, mid 4th century). The angle of the upper wall is less typical but still indicative of a jar which will have appeared in northern Britain late in the importing period. AT. LVII.

185.   Mortarium in very abraded white fabric, probably from Mancetter-Hartshill. Cf. Gillam 1970, no.280 (c.A.D. 270-350). AA. XLVIII.

186.   Flanged and beaded bowl in Black-burnished ware; cf. Gillam 1976, no.45 (late 3rd century). AZ. XLVII.

187.   Flanged and beaded bowl in Black-burnished ware; cf. Gillam
        1976, no.47 (early 4th century).   AC.   XX.

188.   Flanged and beaded bowl in light grey fabric probably of
        East Yorkshire origin; cf. Crambeck (Corder 1937) type 1
        (mid to late fourth century). Perhaps the latest piece of
        pottery so far known from the Civil Settlement. AN.   VIII.

189.   An unusual flanged and beaded bowl in Black-burnished ware.
        The rim is typical of the flanged and beaded bowls of the
        late 3rd and 4th centuries such as nos. 186-8 above, but
        the decoration would normally be regarded as typically 2nd
        century (cf. Gillam 1976, nos.53-9). A second century
        anomoly is possible but a fourth century 'throw-back' seems
        more probable. BM.   XIII.

c) The Sewerage Scheme, 1976.
By P.V.Webster.

        In this section pottery is reported upon in numerical order
of Field Number (FN). A slightly expanded version of this report
will be placed in the site archive.

i) Cutting I.

FN1:
190.   Flagon in light orange fabric, possibly of Cheshire Plain
        origin. The even rings suggest a late 1st or early 2nd
        century date, cf. Gillam 1970, type 2 (A.D.70-110). AO,
        AR, CY.

FN2:
191.   Flagon in light orange fabric; cf. Holt (Grimes 1930)
        no.127 for the general type. Probably late 1st to early
        2nd century. AS.

192.   Flagon in light fawn-buff fabric. Cf. no.190 above.   CV.

193.   Flagon in orange Cheshire Plain fabric.   AS.

194.   Jar in light orange Cheshire Plain fabric. The fabric
        resembles that common in 2nd-early 3rd century levels at
        Wilderspool (Hinchcliffe forthcoming).   AS.

195.   'Amphora-shaped' small jar in pink-buff Cheshire Plain
        fabric with a grey core. It seems most likely that this
        vessel was intended to fit into a stand or holder.   AS.

196.   Small beaker in light grey Cheshire Plain fabric. It is
        reminiscent of the beakers found in Black-burnished ware

between the mid 2nd and the late 3rd century (cf. Gillam 1970, type 65) and is probably of a similar date. CV.

197.   Jar in smooth mid-grey fabric sooted on the rim. AS.

198.   Jar in grey Cheshire Plain fabric smoothed externally with external sooting. It is reminiscent of mid-late 2nd century vessels in Black-burnished ware (cf. Gillam 1976, no.3) and is probably of a similar date. CV.

199.   Bowl in light orange-red fabric with traces if mica dusting externally. Possibly a Holt product. The overall form may have resembled Holt (Grimes 1930) no.92. Late 1st - early/ mid 2nd century. AS.

200.   Flanged and grooved bowl or dish in Black-burnished ware. The fragment is small but it is probably part of a vessel such as Gillam 1976, no.42. Late 2nd -early 3rd century.

202.   Mortarium in orange-buff fabric. BJ.

203.   Mortarium in orange-red fabric with a white calcitic filler. AS.

FN2 contained plentiful 2nd century pottery. One sherd (no. 200) suggests that deposition did not take place before the later years of the century.

FN5:
204.   (Not illustrated). Neck sherd of a flagon in Black-burnished ware with the distinctive vertical burnishing of this class of vessel. For a possible reconstruction see Webster 1982, p.31. Examples of this type of vessel in the north date from the 2nd and early 3rd century. See also nos. 206 & 220 below and Wallace & Webster 1987. CW.

205.   (Not illustrated). Abraded sherd of flanged and ridged bowl in East Yorkshire fabric, probably Crambeck ware, see Corder 1937, type 1. c.A.D.350-400. CW.

FN9:
206.   Flagon in Black-burnished ware; cf. no. 204 above. DA.

207.   Jar in Black-burnished ware; cf. Gillam 1970, type 118 (A.D. 120-160). DA.

208.   Flanged bowl or dish in Black-burnished ware. One of the Hadrianic-Antonine series. DA.

FN20, Layer A:
209.   Two-handled flagon in orange-buff Cheshire Plain fabric; see Holt (Grimes 1930), no.127 for the general type (late 1st - early 2nd century. DB.

ii) **Cutting II.**

FN215:
210.   Jar in light orange-buff fabric, sooted on the rim.   A2.

FN218:
211.   (Not illustrated). Rim of dish in mid grey fabric.

FN228:
212.   Flagon in fairly soft orange fabric. The even rings suggest
        a 1st or early 2nd century date.   DF.

213.   Flanged bowl in pink-buff fabric with a grey core. EC.

FN232:
214:    Jar in grey-brown fabric; Gillam 1970, type 166 (A.D.
        70-110) has similarities.   DN.

215.   Flanged and reeded bowl in orange-buff fabric with a grey
        core; cf. Holt (Grimes 1930) no.85 (late 1st - early 2nd
        century).   DN.

FN234:
216.   (Not illustrated). Five sherds of a jar in cream to
        pink-buff fabric decorated with applied dots and circles in
        pink slip as Gillam 1970, type 68. Late 1st - early 2nd
        century.   DQ.

FN243:
217.   Jar in gritty grey-brown fabric with rusticated decoration;
        cf. Gillam 1970, type 97 (A.D.80-130).   DX.

218.   Jar in orange fabric heavily sooted in use. The drawing is
        reconstructed from numerous fragments, not all joining.
        EI.

iii) **Cutting III.**

FN300:
219.   Beaker in very pale orange-buff fabric with a grey-brown
        colour coat possibly from a beaker such as Gillam 1970,
        type 52 (A.D. 250-300).   CH.

220.   Flagon in Black-burnished ware. The handle has been fixed
        at its lower end by fashioning a lug to the handle, poking
        a hole through the body of the pot and inserting the
        handle. The resultant joint has been smoothed on the
        outside only. Cf. no.204 above.   AG.

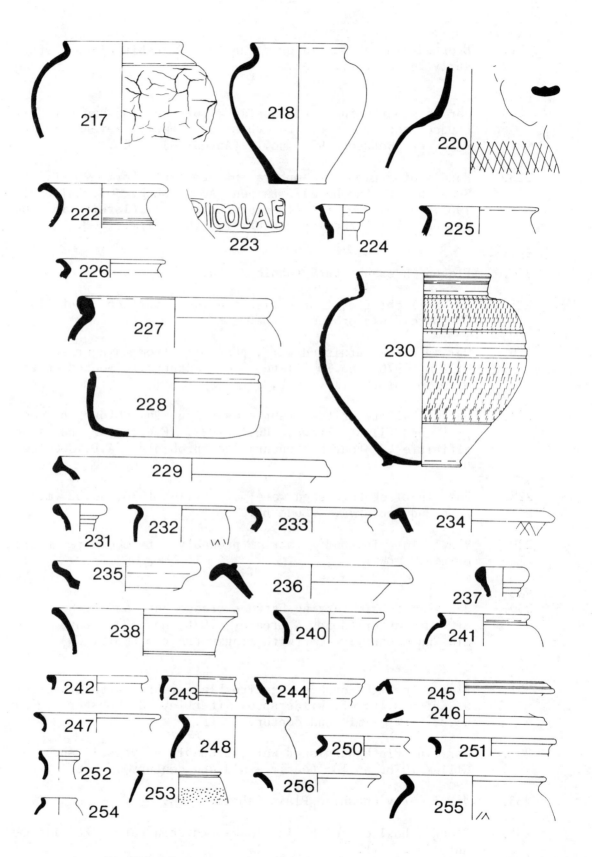

Fig.16. Coarse pottery nos. 217-8, 220, 222-256.
Scale 1:4 (except 223 - 1:2).

FN307:
221.   Everted rim jar in mid grey fabric. Probably late 1st -
        early 2nd century.   AF.

FN315:
222.   Jar in smooth pink-buff fabric.   Soil action has entirely
        eroded the surface, but this is probably Severn Valley
        Ware, cf. Webster 1977, no.11 (Antonine).   CL.

223.   Handle of a globular amphora of Dressel form 20 (South
        Spanish oil amphora) stamped AG]RICOLAE. Cf. Callender
        1965, p.66, no.51. Callender suggests a **floruit** in the
        second half of the 1st century for this firm.   CQ.

FN317:
224.   Flagon in orange-buff fabric.   BW.

225.   Jar in light grey fabric with a darker surface; probably a
        Cheshire Plain product.   BW.

226.   Jar in Black-burnished ware; possibly from a jar such as
        Gillam 1976, no.18 (late 3rd century).   Sooted on the
        exterior of the rim.   BW.

227.   Jar in Calcite gritted fabric varying in colour between
        grey and light brown; Hull 1932, Fig.15, 2 has some
        affinities.   Fourth century and probably c.A.D. 360-400.
        BP.

228.   Bowl in Black-burnished ware; cf. Gillam 1976, no.52 (mid -
        late 2nd century).   BU & BP.

229.   ?Bowl in pink-buff fabric probably of Cheshire Plain
        origin.   BW.

FN318:
230.   Jar in a fabric varying between orange-buff and light grey;
        cf. Manchester (Jones & Grealey 1974, no.152). Late 1st -
        mid 2nd century.   CM (with fragments from FN319, CN).

FN319:
231.   Flagon in light orange Cheshire Plain fabric with traces of
        a white slip; cf. Wilderspool (Hartley & Webster 1973)
        no.3. Early - mid 2nd century.   EL.

232.   Jar in Black-burnished ware; probably a vessel such as
        Gillam 1976, no.13 (early - mid 4th century).   EL.

233.   Jar in grey Cheshire Plain fabric.   CN.

234.   Flanged bowl or dish in Black-burnished ware. Hadrianic-
        Antonine.   EL.

235.   Dish in Black-burnished ware.   The form may be derived from the Belgic platter, Camulodunum type 8 (Hawkes & Hull 1947), but is not one to be expected in this fabric or in this area.   CN.

FN321:
236.   (Not illustrated).   Neck sherd of a flagon in Black-burnished ware. cf. no.204 above.   AH.

237.   Flagon in off-white fabric; cf. Gillam 1970, type 5 (A.D. 110-130).   AH.

238.   ?Jar in orange-buff fabric with a light red core. Possibly Severn Valley Ware.   See Webster 1976, no.1 for the general type.   AH.

239.   (Not illustrated).   Body sherd of a beaker in cream fabric with a rose-pink colour coat; probably a Nene Valley product.   It is decorated with barbotine strands and is

probably from a beaker such as Gillam 1970, type 80 (3rd century).   AD.

FN323:
240.   Jar in grey fabric.   EU.

241.   Jar in grey fabric.   There is some resemblance to the Black-burnished jar Gillam 1970, type 124 and this piece could well be of a similar date (Hadrianic to Antonine). EU.

iv) **Cutting IV.**

FN600:
All vessels from this level were severely eroded by soil action.

242.   Jar in grey fabric probably of Cheshire Plain origin; cf. Wilderspool (Hartley & Webster 1973) no.9 for a possible reconstruction. 2nd century.   GG.

243.   Jar in light red fabric.

244.   Bowl in pink-buff fabric, reminiscent of the samian form 27 and probably, like it, pre-c.A.D.150.   GG

245.   Flanged bowl in pink to fawn fabric; one of the late 1st to early 2nd century series.   GG.

246.   Lid in fawn Cheshire Plain fabric.   GG.

FN601:

247.   Jar in light grey fabric, probably of Cheshire Plain origin. GH.

248.   Jar in light grey fabric with a darker surface. GH.

249.   (Not illustrated). Wall sherds of a jar in Black-burnished ware with acute angled lattice. Probably 2nd century. GH.

FN603:

250.   Jar in light grey fabric; cf. Gillam 1970, type 102 (A.D. 80-120). GI.

251.   Jar in light grey Cheshire Plain fabric with a darker surface. GI.

FN604:

This feature is thought to be a disturbance in the Roman ground surface and as it contained a piece of asbestos it must be regarded as modern. However, all the pottery from it was Roman and two sherds are illustrated below.

252.   Flagon in orange-buff fabric; cf. Corbridge 'destruction deposit', Richmond & Gillam 1950, no.3 (late 2nd century). HO.

253.   Rough cast beaker in off-white fabric with a light red-brown colour coat externally and a grey-brown colour coat internally. Vessels such as this may come from the Nene Valley industry , cf. Great Casterton (Corder 1961) no.2 but are more likely to be from Koln cf. Anderson 1981, fig. 19.1, nos. 5-6. Anderson would date these beakers c.A.D. 80-150/60 but a date in the mid 2nd century seems more likely for the examples from northern Britain. HO.

FN607:

254.   Small pot in light orange Cheshire Plain fabric. HP.

255.   Jar in Black-burnished ware; cf. Gillam 1976, no.4 (late 2nd century). HP.

256.   Jar in Black-burnished ware; cf. Gillam 1976, no.10 (late 3rd century). HP.

257.   Lid in grey fabric. HP.

FN610.

258.   Flagon in orange fabric with a grey core; cf. Gillam 1970, type 5 (A.D.110-150). GP.

259.   Beaker in light brown fabric with a grey core and grey

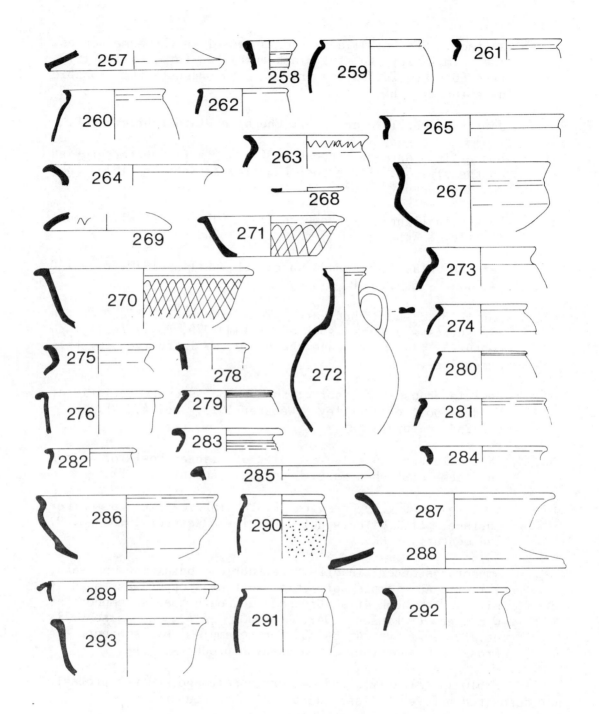

Fig.17. Coarse pottery nos. 257-293. Scale 1:4.

surface. See no.241 above for a vessel in the same series.
The similarity to the Black-burnished form, Gillam 1970,
type 66 (late 2nd to mid 3rd century) suggests the probable
date range. HK.

260.   Jar or beaker in orange-buff Cheshire Plain fabric. GP.

261.   Beaker in orange-buff Cheshire Plain fabric burnt greyish
        on the rim; cf. Wilderspool (Hartley & Webster 1973) no.
        28. 2nd century. GP.

262.   Beaker in light grey Cheshire Plain fabric; cf. Wilderspool
        (Hartley & Webster 1973) nos. 23-4. 2nd century. GP.

263.   Jar in Black-burnished ware; cf. Gillam 1970, type 120
        (A.D. 120-160). GP.

264.   Jar in Black-burnished ware. The pronounced flare of the
        rim suggests a vessel such as Gillam 1976, no.12 (early 4th
        century) in which case the piece is intrusive in this
        assemblage. HK.

265.   Bowl in orange-buff fabric; the shape is characteristic of
        Wilderspool, cf. Hartley & Webster 1973, no.54. Probably
        mid 2nd century. HK.

266.   (Not illustrated). Two examples of flanged bowls or dishes
        in Black-burnbished ware. Hadrianic-Antonine. HK.

267.   Bowl in light grey Cheshire Plain fabric with a darker
        surface; cf. Wilderspool (Hartley & Webster 1973) no.49.
        2nd century. HK.

268.   Amphora stopper in off-white fabric containing a sandy
        filler. An example of this sort of stopper was found **in
        situ** in the neck of a Dressel 20 South Spanish amphora at
        Wroxeter (Atkinson 1942, Fig.43, A14). See also Colls
        et.al. 1977, pp.24, 34, 39 for examples of stoppers in
        Dressel 20 and other South Spanish products. HK.

        FN610 is clearly a 2nd century assemblage and was probably
not deposited before the last quarter of that century.

FN632 (= FN610, layer B):
269.   Lid in Black-burnished ware. For a likely reconstruction
        of the type see Holt (Grimes 1930) no.100. GQ.

FN612:
270.   Flanged bowl in Black-burnished ware; cf. Gillam 1976,
        no.35 (mid 2nd century). HL.

271.   Flanged dish in Black-burnished ware. One of the
        Hadrianic-Antonine series. HL.

FN629:
272.   Flagon in light red fabric probably of Cheshire Plain origin; see Holt (Grimes 1930) no.112 (early/mid 2nd century?).   HT.

273.   Jar in Black-burnished ware, heavily sooted externally; cf. Gillam 1970, type 120 (A.D. 120-160).   GL.

274.   Jar in light grey Cheshire Plain fabric with a darker surface. The bulbous shape suggests a late 1st to early 2nd century date.   GO.

275.   Jar in Black-burnished ware burnt light grey to orange; cf. Gillam 1976, no.5 (late 2nd to early 3rd century).   GL.

276.   Flanged bowl in fawn fabric. One of three flanged bowls of pre-Hadrianic type from this level.   GL.

277.   (Not illustrated). Flanged bowl in Black-burnished ware. One of the Hadrianic-Antonine series.   GL.

FN632:   see no.269 above.

FN633:
278.   Flagon neck in smooth orange fabric.   HC.

279.   Beaker in light red-brown fabric; cf. Wilderspool (Hartley & Webster 1973), no.31. Early - mid 2nd century.   HU.

280.   Beaker in light brown Cheshire Plain fabric; cf. Wilderspool (Hartley & Webster 1973) no.23. Early - mid 2nd century.   HC

281.   Beaker in light brown Cheshire Plain fabric; cf. Wilderspool (Hartley & Webster 1973) no.37. Early - mid 2nd century.   HC.

282.   Beaker in orange-buff Cheshire Plain fabric; cf. Wilderspool (Hartley & Webster 1973) nos.24-5. Early - mid 2nd century. HU.

283.   Jar in light grey Cheshire Plain fabric.   HC.

284.   Jar in Black-burnished ware, sooted on the rim externally; cf. Gillam 1976, no.2 (mid 2nd century). HU.

285.   Flanged dish or bowl in abraded grey fabric with a dark grey coat. Probably Black-burnished ware Category 2; cf. Gillam 1970, type 310 (c.A.D. 150-210).   HC.

286.   Bowl in light grey Cheshire Plain fabric; cf. Wilderspool (Hartley & Webster 1973) nos. 54-5. Mid 2nd century. HU.

287.   Flared bowl in light grey Cheshire Plain fabric.   HU.

288. Lid in buff fabric.   HC.

There is a high proportion of pottery from the Cheshire Plain (and much of it probably from Wilderspool) in this feature. An early – mid 2nd century date seems assured for the collection. Deposition was probably in the mid 2nd century.

FN637:
289.   Flanged bowl in light orange Cheshire Plain fabric; cf. Holt (Grimes 1930) nos. 83–8. Late 1st to early 2nd century. HA.

FN700, layer 3:
290.   Rough cast beaker burnt fawn grey. Cf. Gillam 1970, types 72–6, Anderson 1981, Fig. 19.3, nos.25–6, 28–9 for the general type which is probably of North Gaulish origin. Probably late 1st to mid 2nd century.   GR.

291.   Beaker or small jar in Black–burnished ware; cf. Gillam 1976, no.24 (early – mid 2nd century).   GR.

292.   Jar in Black–burnished ware burnt light grey to pink; cf. Gillam 1976, no. 4 (late 2nd century).   GR.

293.   Flanged bowl in dark grey fabric; peraps of a similar type to Gillam 1970, no.218 (early – mid 2nd century).   GR.

v) Unstratified pottery.

As would be expected from the nature of the sewerage scheme operation, large numbers of unstratified sherds were recovered. A report on the more unusual of these together with unreduced drawings will be placed in the site archive. The archive will also contain a report on material from **Cutting I Extension.**

d) The Sheltered Housing, 1980
By R.C.Turner.

The volume of Roman coarse pottery recovered from this excavation was very small in relation to the area and depth of deposits.   This, together with the general lack of other dating material has made it hard to date the separate structural events. Consequently the coarse pottery has been arranged in the same order as the descriptive text (Part 2 of this series, Chapter 4). The context and catalogue numbers appear after each description. The site code, to be found on all pottery is RB80.

i) Earliest Roman features.

The bulk of the coarse pottery from these features comes

from the upper levels of the early ditch and its immediate surroundings. All the datable material is pre-A.D. 130 and there is no Black-burnished ware present. These features were probably filled by c.A.D. 120.

300.   Ring-necked flagon in smooth, pale orange fabric with a three-element strap handle; cf. Gillam 1970, type 2 (A.D. 70-110).   66/1.

301.   Beaker in soft orange fabric with a light grey core and exterior surface; cf. Gillam 1970, type 97 (A.D. 80-120). 66/2.

302.   Jar in hard light grey fabric with a mid-grey surface and traces of mica dusting. The shoulder shows two horizontal grooves; cf. Gillam 1970, type 108 (A.D. 80-130). 97/1.

303.   Nearly complete rusticated beaker in a hard sandy light grey fabric; cf. Gillam 1970, type 98 (A.D. 80-130). 66/3.

ii) Roman timber building.

The fills of the structural elements of this building yielded only 13 sherds of coarse pottery, including one rim of a second century Black-burnished ware jar.

iii) Industrial pits and gullies.

This phase of activity produced an appreciable group of coarse pottery with little residual material. The high proportion of mortaria is striking. The group is late Antonine.

304.   Jar in Black-burnished ware; cf. Gillam 1976, no.4 (late 2nd century).   45/1.

305.   Mortarium in a brick-red sandy fabric with multicoloured grits; cf. Gillam 1970, type 257 (A.D. 160-200).   44/1.

306.   Mortarium in an orange sandy fabric with a pinker core and mixed grey and white quartzite grits; cf. Gillam 1970, type 257 and Hartley & Webster 1973, no.103. Antonine. 45/2.

307.   A worn mortarium in a fine-textured cream fabric with some fine quartz, red-brown and blackish inclusions and much blackish and occasional red-brown trituration grit. Two attempts have been made at impressing the stamp which is both smudged and incomplete. Clear impressions, however, show it to be an illiterate stamp. Stamps from the same die have been recorded from Alcester, Bannaventa (Whilton Lodge), Olney, Bucks., Ribchester, Manduessedum (at least 5), Templeborough and Wroxeter. The potter can be attributed to the Mancetter (Manduessedum) – Hartshill

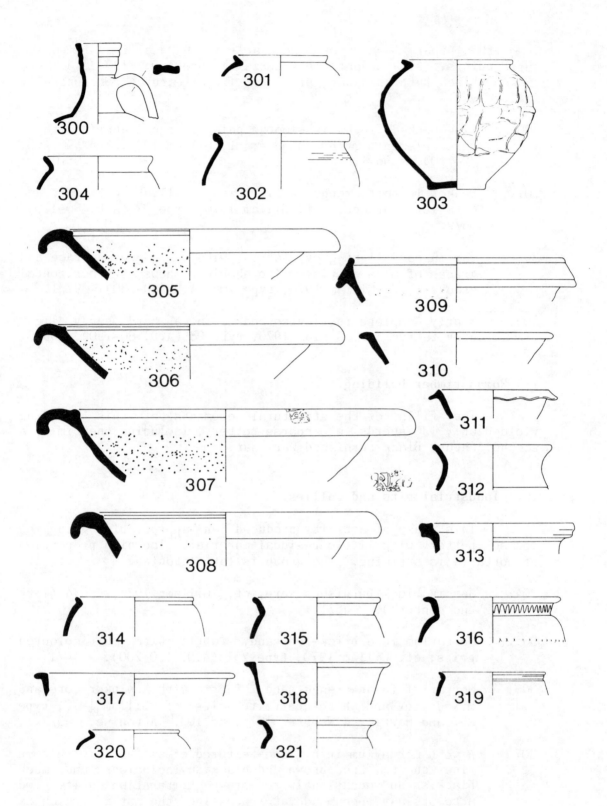

Fig.18. Coarse pottery nos. 300–321. Scale 1:4.

potteries, though his kilns have not been found. The rim forms indicate a date within the period A.D. 120-160. (KFH) 44/3.

308.   Mortarium in an orange-pink sandy fabric with a lighter core and large white and grey quartzite grits; cf. Hartley & Webster 1973, no.101. Hadrianic-Antonine. 44/2.

309.   Hammer-head mortarium in a soft buff fabric with medium sized grey grits. It is similar to Gillam 1970, type 259 (A.D. 160-200) but probably of a slightly later form. 25/1.

310.   Flat-rimmed dish in Black-burnished ware; cf. Gillam 1976, no.64 (mid-late 2nd century). 45/3.

311.   Tazza in smooth soft orange fabric; cf. Gillam 1970, type 347 (A.D. 140-200). 45/4.

The following group came from context 43, an horizon sealing most of the pits and showing a range of types broadly contemporary with nos. 304-311 above:

312.   Part of what appear to be two storage jars of which the rim survives for only one. This piece is in a hard red-buff fabric with a light grey core exterior surfaces. Severn Valley Ware, see Webster 1977, nos. 4 & 16 (c.A.D. 140-160). 43/1.

313.   Storage jar in an orange sandy fabric with traces of buff-orange slip. 43/2.

314.   Beaker in Black-burnished ware; cf. Gillam 1976, no.30 (early-mid 2nd century). 43/7.

315.   Jar in Black-burnished ware; cf. Gillam 1976, no.2 (mid 2nd century). 43/3.

316.   Jar in Black-burnished ware with a wavy line around the neck and acute-angled lattice decoration on the body; cf. Gillam 1976, no.3 (mid-late 2nd century). 43/4.

317.   Flat-rimmed bowl in Black-burnished ware. Mid 2nd century. 43/5.

318.   Small flat-rimmed bowl in a pale orange sandy fabric with a light grey core. 43/6.

iv) **The defences.**

Unfortunately the volume of pottery recovered from this complicated sequence is insufficient to establish a firm chronology. The vessels illustrated are arranged in structural sequence.

319. Beaker in a coarse buff-orange fabric perhaps from Wilderspool. Probably an imitation of North Gaulish rough-cast types. Pre-defence timber foundation trench. 115/1.

320. Beaker in a soft light grey fabric. c.A.D. 80-130. Pre-defence timber foundation trench. 115/2.

321. Jar in Black-burnished ware; cf. Gillam 1970, type 138 (A.D. 150-250). Pre-defence timber foundation trench. 115/3.

322. Ring-necked flagon in a hard orange sandy fabric with the remains of a single strap handle; cf. Gillam 1970, type 2 (A.D. 70-110). Early rampart. 92/1.

323. Ring-necked flagon in a smooth coffee-coloured fabric with a two-element strap handle. The piece is a partial waster. Cf. Gillam 1970, type 2 (A.D. 70-110). Fill of shelf. 132/1.

324. Jar in Black-burnished ware; cf. Gillam 1976, no.4 (late 2nd century). Primary silt of phase 1 ditch. 110/1.

325. Mortarium in hard orange-pink fabric with traces of a cream slip; cf. Gillam 1970, types 256/8 (A.D. 150-200). Primary silt of phase 1 ditch. 110/2.

326. Mortarium in soft cream fabric with medium sized black trituration grits; cf. Gillam 1970, type 264 (A.D. 180-200). Later rampart. 10/1.

327. Beaker in a soft light grey fabric with an orange interior. A.D. 80-130. Fill of phase 2 ditch depression. 30/1.

328. Jar in Black-burnished war with wavy line decoration on the neck. Mid-late 2nd century. Fill of phase 2 ditch/ depression. 30/2.

329. Mortarium in a hard orange sandy fabric with a light grey core; cf. Hartley & Webster 1973, no. 115, Gillam 1970, type 245 (A.D. 110-160). Fill of phase 2 ditch/depression. 30/3.

330. Plain-rimmed bowl in Black-burnished ware; cf. Gillam 1976, no.75 (early-mid 2nd century). Fill of phase 2 ditch/depression. 30/4.

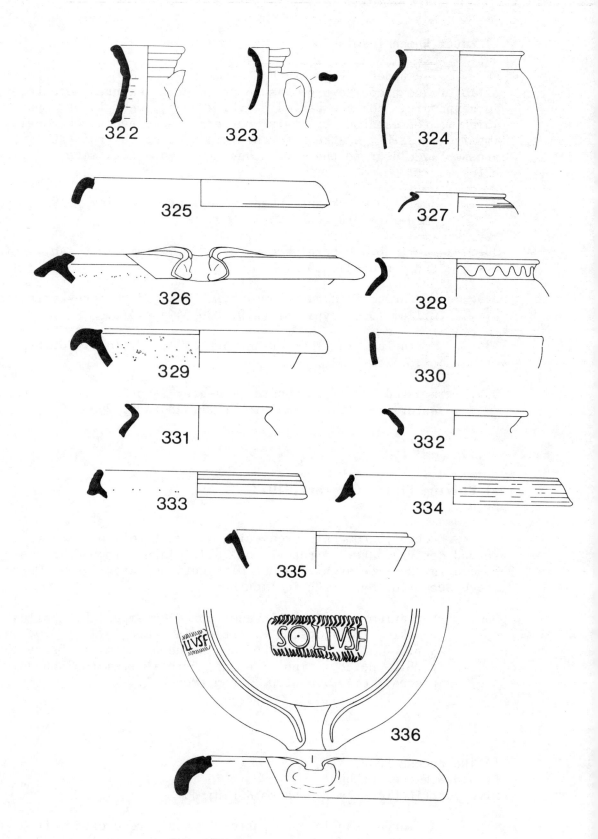

Fig.19. Coarse pottery nos. 322–336.
Scale 1:4 (except stamp – 1:2).

v) **Later Roman levels.**

The upper levels of the site have produced a thin scatter of later Roman coarseware. As no structural features were recorded corresponding to the period c.A.D. 200-350, the latter part of which is represented by this pottery, some nearby occupation is implied, possibly adjacent to the main road north from the fort but presumably closer to the fort that the Car Park site, section e below.

331.   Jar in Black-burnished ware; cf. Gillam 1976, no.9 (mid-late 3rd century). 6/1.

332.   Jar in Black-burnished ware; cf. Gillam 1976, no.10 (late 3rd century). 5/1.

333.   Mortarium in hard cream fabric with dark grey grits; cf. Gillam 1970, type 281 (A.D. 230-340). 5/2.

334.   Mortarium in soft cream fabric; cf. Gillam 1970, type 284 (A.D. 280-360). 5/3.

335.   Flanged bowl in a hard mid-grey fabric with a darker exterior; cf. Gillam 1970, type 228 (A.D. 290-370). 58/1.

e) **Playing Fields Car Park, 1973.**
By P.V.Webster.

Pottery from this excavation was uniformly of late first to second century date. A report on all diagnostic pieces has been placed in the site archive along with outline drawings. Only one piece seems worthy of publication here:

336.   Mortarium in granular cream fabric stamped by Sollus of Brockley Hill; cf. K.F.Hartley in Frere 1972, p.379, no.38 & p.377, fig.146; also an amended date in Frere 1984, p.281, no.38. The drawing here is from two non-joining pieces. c.A.D. 60-100. From trench A.

f) **The Access Road.**
By J.H.S.Witherington.
With contributions by P.Gibbons & L.Hird.

A large sample of pottery was recovered from the excavations, 85% of which was stratified. In total 8,503 sherds were noted, representing a minimum of c.1200 vessels. An approximate division of vessels by class is shown below:

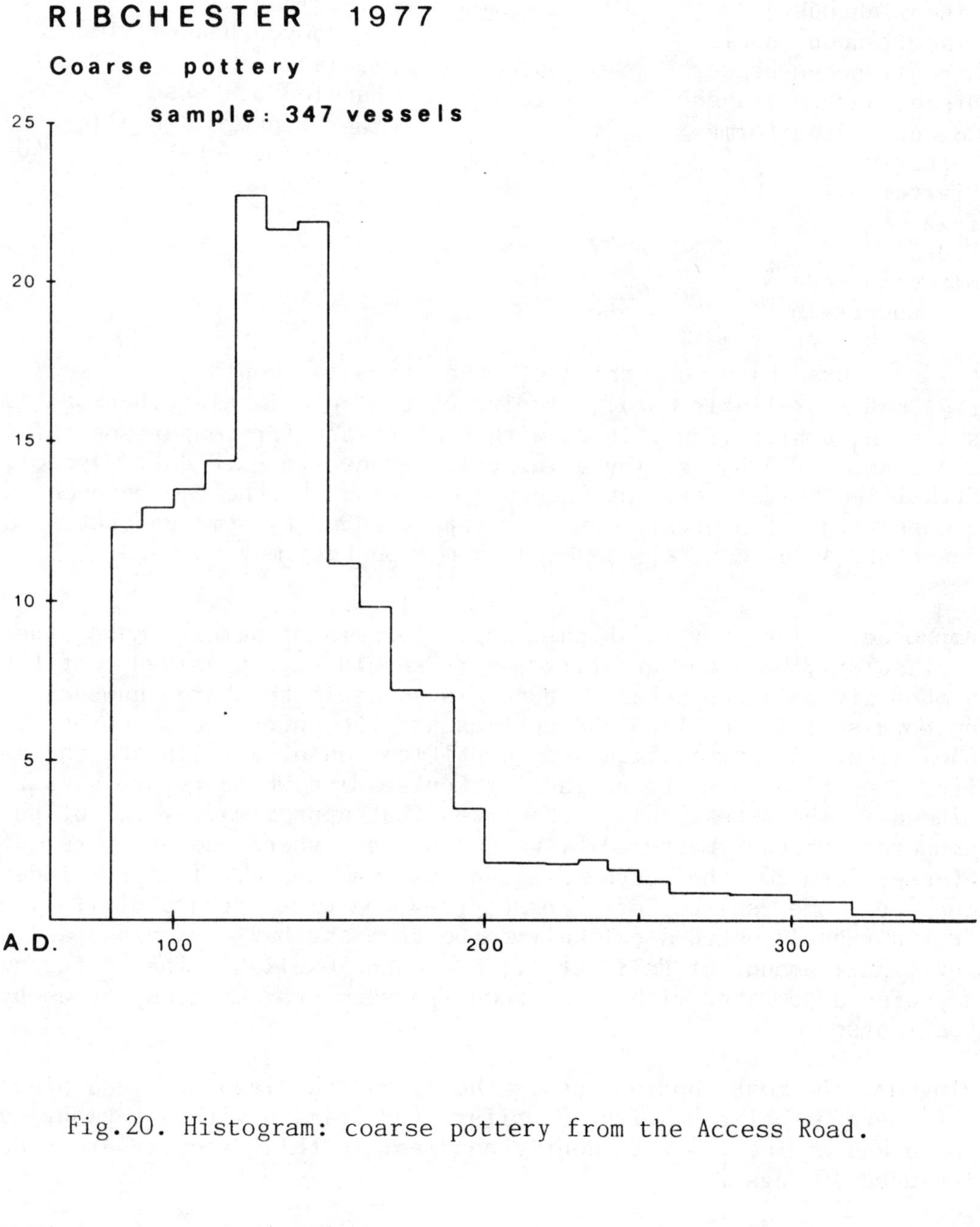

RIBCHESTER 1977

Coarse pottery

sample: 347 vessels

Fig.20. Histogram: coarse pottery from the Access Road.

Amphorae	100	Black-burnished ware:	
Flagons	139	Jars	114
Greyware jars	46	Dishes:	
Rusticated jars	82	Flat-rim	85
Miscellaneous jars	102	Plain rim	22
Miscellaneous bowls	75	Grooved/beaded rim	20
Miscellaneous beakers	76	Bowls	75
Miscellaneous dishes	8	Handled beakers	8
Colour-coated forms	71	Other beakers & small	
Mortaria	95	cooking pots	40
Platters	4		
Tazza	1		
Lids	37		
Miscellaneous & uncertain	45		

Less than one third of the vessels could be given a reasonably reliable date. Their chronological distribution is shown in a histogram (Fig.20 with samian ware for comparison, Fig. 21) constructed by giving a value in decades to each dated vessel. Stratified vessels are catalogued according to their occurence in groups within features. These are supplemented by some unstratified material. A few general comments on the pottery may be made:

Amphorae. The way in which these vessels fragment make them particularly hard to quantify and it should be emphasised that the number given in the chart above is an estimate. Large numbers of amphora sherds came from the cobbles at the north-east corner of the site. An examination and quantification of all amphora sherds from the site has been made by Louise Hird whose report will be placed in the site archive. She notes that approximately 95% of the amphorae (whether measured by weight or by sherd count) are of Dressel form 20, the South Spanish oil amphorae. The remainder include some sherds of Dressel 2-4, a wine amphora of Italian origin (sherds noted are likely to be from the Bay of Naples) and a very small amount of Pelichet 47, a South Gaulish wine amphora. Amphorae associated with fish products seem to be conspicuous by their absence.

Flagons. The most common type is the ring-neck flagon (19 examples) but there are also 8 with a bifurcated rim, 4 with a cup-shaped mouth and at least 4 with double handles. In this category are also included 10 jugs.

Black-burnished ware. The fabric is Gillam's Category 1 (1970) although there are some variants, also handmade; for a full discussion of these fabrics see Williams 1977. Vessels in Black-burnished ware account for over 30% of the total sample. A breakdown by type and date will be placed in the site archive. Only 4 of the 145 datable Black-burnished ware vessels belong to the third century and none to the fourth. Of the jars, nearly 60% are datable to the early to mid second century, with vessels possessing the rounded contours of Gillam 1970, type 122 being well represented. The earlier types of flat-rim dish are more numerous

RIBCHESTER   1977

Dated   samian   (sample: 774 vessels)

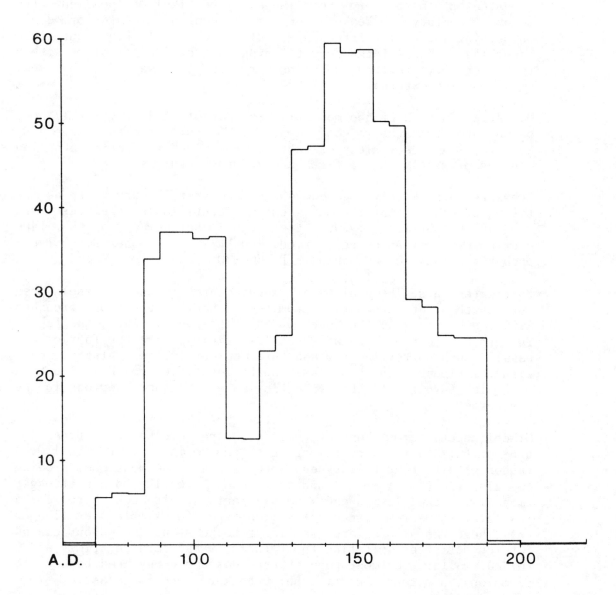

Fig.21. Histogram: samian ware fom the Access Road.

than the later types and the flanged and beaded dishes which replaced them are not in evidence at all. A minority of dishes had plain, beaded or grooved rims. Of the plain rim dishes, 12 were without lattice decoration, 7 with it; intersecting arc decoration was found on 2 examples. Of the 75 bowls identified, only 15 could be dated but there were no flanged types likely to post-date the second century. Beakers or small cooking pots formed a surprisingly high percentage of the total Black-burnished assemblage. These forms seem to favour a grey fabric, often with a rather crumbly texture and some were very thin walled with a very smooth polish externally.

Mortaria. Only 20 of the mortaria were datable and of these 17 need be no later than the second century; 3 fall into the range A.D. 230-340. A wide variety of fabrics were noted reflecting changing sources of supply in the first and second centuries.

Greyware jars. Rarely does enough of the profile survive to define types precisely but the most common identifiable examples were similar to Gillam 1970, types 115-7 belonging to the late Hadrianic/ early Antonine period. The bulk of the sherds, however, probably belong to the period A.D. 80-130.

Rusticated jars. The quality of manufacture in these vessels does not match that of examples from the School foundation trenches (section h below) to the South of the Bath-house. There the fabric is hard and often has a sheen-like finish; here the fabrics are usually much softer in grey and buff colours. The relative ease with which sherds in this class can be identified may have led to a bias in favour of the late Flavian and Trajanic periods in the histogram.

Miscellaneous forms. Many of the jars are everted-rim types, in grey or buff fabrics and belonging to the period c.A.D. 80-130. A number of different bowl types were found, the most common being the flat rim (16 examples) and the reeded rim (10), again strongly emphasising the Flavian and Trajanic periods, although there were a few later forms reminiscent of samian types (8 examples) or flanged (5). There was also a large sample of beakers, not in colour coated fabrics but often imitating their forms; 9 had cornice rims and 6 folded walls; the most popular type was the poppy-head beaker (16 examples), a second century type; 6 beakers were roughcast.

Other categories. Numerous colour coated forms were found in Colchester, Nene Valley and 'Rhenish' fabrics. Lids too were relatively well represented, the majority being in grey fabrics. Remaining forms include a tazza, platters, storage jars, a cheese ring, an unguentarium and the base of a triple vase.

The very large quantity of pottery from this excavation has necessitated a slightly more abbreviated catalogue than that originally prepared. The original version which contains some further fabric details and expanded details of vessels refered to below but not illustrated or catalogued will be placed in the site archive.

Below stone building (Section P-Q, 7).
340.   Bowl or tankard in a dull orange fabric. GT.1.

Wall of the stone building (Section P-Q, 5).
341.   Bowl with grooved rim in Black-burnished ware. DL.1.

Stone building (Section P-Q, 3 & 4).
342.   Ring-neck flagon in a soft orange fabric with traces of a white slip. FQ.17.

343.   Narrow-mouthed jar in a soft 'soapy' grey fabric; cf. Gillam 1970, types 30-2 (late 2nd century). FE.6.

344.   Narrow-mouthed jar in a soft gritty grey fabric. FE.4.

345.   Jar in a hard gritty grey fabric with roughcast decoration. GX.1.

346.   Jar in Black-burnished ware. FQ.25.

347.   Jar in Black-burnished ware; cf. Gillam 1976, no.9 (mid-late 3rd century). FQ.20.

348.   Beaker in Black-burnished ware. GX.6.

349.   Bead rim jar in Black-burnished ware. Mid to late 2nd century. FQ.29.

350.   Beaker in Black-burnished ware. FE.1.

351.   Bead-rim jar in Black-burnished ware. FQ.22.

352.   Large bag-shaped beaker with a cornice rim in a soft orange-brown fabric with roughcast exterior. Possibly a Wilderspool product. FQ.7.

353.   Carinated beaker in a soft red-brown fabric with a darker exterior. FP.24.

354.   Mortarium (diameter c.34 cms.) in a fairly fine-textured cream fabric with a little very fine quartz and red-brown tempering; no trituration grit survives. The broken stamp is from one of seven dies of Sarrius and this mortarium is a product of his Warwickshire workshop. Twenty-eight of

his stamps are recorded from Scotland and eighty-two from sites in England, excluding the two pottery-making sites at Mancetter-Hartshill, Warks. and Rossington Bridge, near Doncaster, where he had workshops which were almost certainly partly contemporary. A stamp from Birdoswald is from a deposit dated c.A.D. 125-140 (Richmond & Birley 1930, p.187, no.2 - described as an illiterate stamp but in fact from the same die as the Ribchester stamp), but the large number of stamps from Antonine deposits in Scotland and one from a Verulamium deposit dated A.D. 155-160 (Frere 1972, p.378, no.35) point to a mainly Antonine date. The period c.A.D. 135-165/170 should cover his activity. Sarrius was the most prolific potter stamping mortaria in Britain in the second century. (KFH) FP.33.

355. Flat-rimmed bowl in Black-burnished ware; cf. Gillam 1976, no.36 (mid 2nd century). FP.1.

356. Flat-rimmed bowl in Black-burnished ware; cf. Gillam 1976, nos.35-7 (mid 2nd century). FP.12.

357. Flat-rimmed dish in Black-burnished ware; cf. Gillam 1976, no.57 (early to mid 2nd century). FP.17.

358. Flat-rimmed dish in Black-burnished ware. Mid 2nd century. FE.5. One of two examples.

359. Dish with grooved rim in Black-burnished ware. FE.15. Part of the same vessel came from the same context as nos. 362-383 below.

360. Bowl in soft orange-pink fabric. Possibly a Wilderspool product, cf. Hartley & Webster 1973, nos.54-5. FP.31.

361. Handled beaker in a soft orange fabric. FQ.12.

This context also contained a number of vessels closely similar to some to be illustrated from other parts of the site. These include vessels similar to nos. 366, 371, 481, 486.

Stone Building (section P-Q, 2).
362. Very large, narrow mouthed jar in a hard gritty light grey fabric with brown-grey surfaces. EB.45.

363. Jar in soft gritty grey fabric. EB.7.

364. Everted rim jar in a soft gritty grey fabric. EB.21.

365. Jar in Black-burnished ware with countersunk handles. For the general type see Gillam 1976, no.15 (early - mid 2nd century). EB.25.

366. Jar in Black-burnished ware with wavy line decoration on

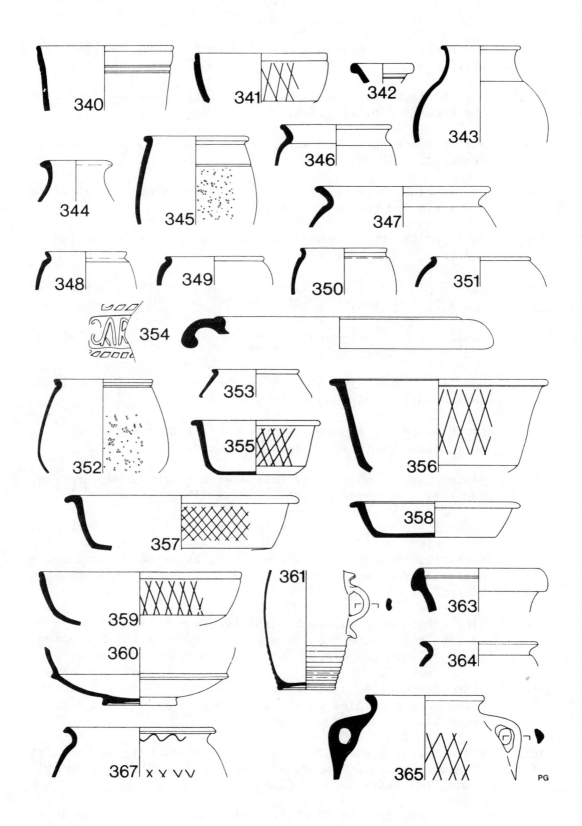

Fig.22. Coarse pottery nos. 340–361, 363–5, 367.
Scale 1:4 (except stamp – 1:2).
Drawn by Paul Gibbons.

the neck: cf. Gillam 1976, no.3 (mid – late 2nd century). EB.46.

367. Jar in Black-burnished ware with wavy line decoration on the neck cf. no.371 below. EB. 33 & 47.

368. Jar in Black-burnished ware; cf. Gillam 1976, no.8 (mid 3rd century). EB.29.

369. Jar in Black-burnished ware; cf. Gillam 1970, no.135 (late 2nd – mid 3rd century). EB.28.

370. Jar in Black-burnished ware with wavy line decoration on the neck. EN.1 & 6.

371. Jar in Black-burnished ware; cf. Gillam 1970, type 122 (c. A.D. 120–160). EB.14.

372. Small jar in Black-burnished ware. There is a graffito on the neck (see archive). EB.37.

372A. Handled beaker in Black-burnished ware; cf. Gillam 1976, no.24 (early – mid 2nd century). EB.57.

373. Large beaker in a soft slightly sandy fabric with roughcast surfaces. Possibly a Wilderspool product. EB.49.

374. Beaker in a soft buff fabric with roughcast decoration. Possibly a Wilderspool product. EB.10.

375. Beaker in a white fabric with blue coating and barbotine decoration. A product of the Nene Valley or, more probably, Koln; cf. Gillam 1970, types 84–5 (late 2nd – early 3rd century). EB.62 with a fragment from the same context as nos. 397–423 below.

376. Flat-rimmed bowl in Black-burnished ware; cf. Gillam 1976, no. 39 (mid – late 2nd century). EB.20 with a fragment from the same context as nos. 397–423 below.

377. Flat-rimmed dish in Black-burnished ware. There are scribed intersecting circles on the base and a slight chamfer on the wall. EB.27 & 38.

378. Flat-rimmed dish in Black-burnished ware. It is smaller than average, but resembles in form Gillam 1976, no.63 (mid –late 2nd century). EB.42.

379. Flat-rimmed dish in Black-burnished ware; cf. Gillam 1976, no.55 (early – mid 2nd century). EB.19.

380. Dish in Black-burnished ware. EB.55.

381. Mortarium (diameter 37 cms.) in hard buff fabric with a

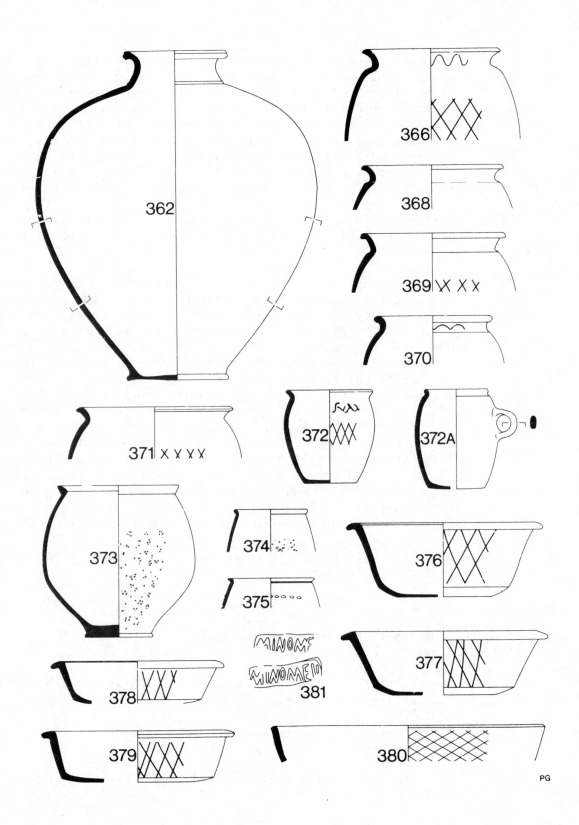

Fig.23. Coarse pottery nos. 362, 366, 368-381.
Scale 1:4 (except 381 - 1:2).
Drawn by Paul Gibbons.

moderate amount of quartz and red-brown tempering. Two stamps from one of the five dies of Minomelus are impressed close together. Four of his mortaria are recorded from Antonine deposits in Scotland and forty from sites in England (excluding those from the kiln sites at Hartshill and Mancetter where he worked). A possible association at one kiln with Vitalis IV suggests that his activity was not solely Antonine and a date of A.D. 130–160 might well cover his activity. (KFH) · EB.35. (Stamp only illustrated).

382. Mortarium in a gritty orange fabric with multicoloured grits. Probably a Wilderspool product; cf. Hartley & Webster 1973, no.109. EB.4.

383. Almost a quarter of a mortarium (diameter 28cms) in soft but slightly granular creamy fabric with a salmon pink core and with a cream inner core; there is much quartz and a very little red-brown tempering. The trituration grit consists of quartz, haematite and ?diorite. The stamp reads BARO and is from the same die as a stamp from Ilkley and one in the Yorkshire Museum, probably found in York or Yorkshire. The potter was probably working in Yorkshire but the location of his workshop is uncertain, although Rossington Bridge is a possibility. The rim forms he used show that he worked within the period c.A.D. 140–190. Although direct evidence is wanting, there are indications that he could be the same Baro who worked at Colchester, apparently without much success (Hull 1963, Fig.60, no.2; Fig.61, nos.2A & 2B). If so, the general indications are that he moved to the North from Colchester. (KFH) EB.5.

Also from this context were vessels closely similar to nos. 346, 516, 529, and fragments of nos. 359, 410 and 458.

From the top layers of the stone building:
384. Flagon or jug in a very hard grey fabric. BC.16.

385. Beaker in a fairly soft smooth black fabric with oxidised buff surfaces in places. DA.1.

386. Tiny beaker in a very abraded soft orange fabric with traces of crude rouletting. CZ.13.

387. Bead-rim dish in Black-burnished ware. Late 2nd century. DX.6.

388. Segmental bowl in a sandy grey-brown fabric with grey surfaces. Closest to Gillam 1970, type 295 (c.A.D. 130–160). BC.4.

389. Dish in a grey-cored fabric with brown margins, granular on the interior, smooth on the exterior surface. BC.15.

390.   Dish in a gritty grey fabric with smooth brown surfaces.
        CZ.4.

391.   Jar in a soft cream fabric with sparsely scattered tiny red
        grits. CZ.6.

392.   Almost a third of a well-worn mortarium (diameter 48 cms)
        in creamy white fabric with a very moderate amount of
        quartz and red-brown tempering; and a fair amount of
        angular red-brown trituration grit. The incompletely
        impressed stamp reads LOCCI.PRO retrograde when complete,
        for a name such as Loccius Proculus or Probus. Ten of his
        mortaria are knowm from Scotland and seventeen from England
        excluding Mancetter where he worked. His activity is dated
        primarily by his stamps from sites of Antonine foundation
        in Scotland while stamps from Benwell and South Shields
        must belong either to the period before A.D.140 or that
        after A.D.158. There is also evidence to show that he
        worked at one time with Iunius Loccius who was probably a
        mid- to late Antonine potter. A date c.A.D. 135-165 is
        indicated. His activity at Mancetter overlapped not only
        with Iunius Loccius but also with Loccius Vibius, with both
        of whom he was surely connected in some way. (KFH). GB.49
        & BC.3.

393.   (Not illustrated). A fragment from a mortarium in fine
        textured cream fabric with quartz and red-brown tempering
        and trituration grit. The potter's stamp is too frag-
        mentary to be identified. The vessel may have been
        manufactured in the Midlands, perhaps in the
        Mancetter-Hartshill potteries in the second century. (KFH)
        BC.13.

There were also vessels similar to nos. 394 below and 356 above.

From the north-west corner of the site (section J-H).
394.   Handled beaker in Black-burnished ware; cf. Gillam 1976,
        nos. 25-6 (mid 2nd century). Section J-H,3. DV.1.

395.   Jar in Black-burnished ware; cf. Gillam 1976, no.4 (late
        2nd century). Section J-H, 3. CA.2.

396.   Plain rimmed dish in Black-burnished ware. Section J-H,
        4. BW.1.

From J-H, 6 came a Black-burnished dish similar to no. 557 below.

From the cobbled area (north-east of site, Section G-F, 5).
397.   Amphora in orange fabric containing black sand. Part of an
        Italian Dressel 2-4 wine amphora. AD.2.

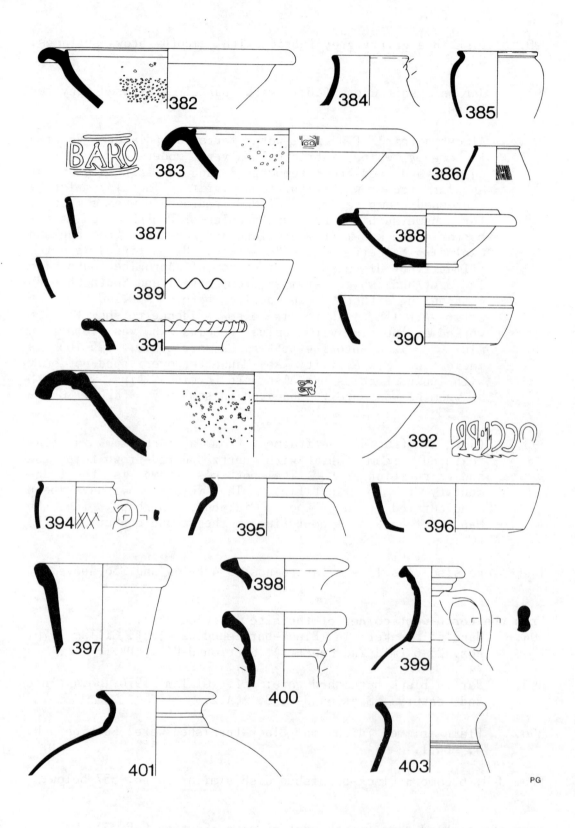

Fig.24. Coarse pottery nos. 382-392. 394-401, 403.
Scale 1:4 (except stamps - 1:2)
Drawn by Paul Gibbons.

398.	Flagon in very hard grey fabric. EP.12.

399.	Ring-neck flagon in a pinky-buff fabric with a white slip. Cf. Gillam 1970, nos.3-4 (late 1st - early/mid 2nd century). GE.37.

400.	Large two-handled flagon in a hard laminar buff fabric. GE.10.

401.	Narrow-mouthed jar in a hard grey-cored red-brown fabric with gritty surfaces. EP.7.

402.	Large wide-mouthed jar in a soft orange-buff fabric. GE.34.

403.	Jar in hard pink fabric with a white slip. GE.36.

404.	Jar in a light grey sandy fabric; cf. Gillam 1970, no.112 (early-mid 2nd century). FR.10 & GE.3.

405.	Jar in Black-burnished ware; similar to Gillam 1970, type 133 (mid/late 2nd - early 3rd century). CP.9.

406.	Jar in Black-burnished ware. GE.15.

407.	Small jar in Black-burnished ware. A graffito on this vessel is reported in the archive. EO.9.

408.	Small jar in Black-burnished ware. GE.12.

409.	Beaker in slightly sandy dark grey fabric. GE.42.

410.	Bowl or dish in Black-burnished ware. Part of the same vessel came from the same context as nos. 362-383 above. BZ.1.

411.	Dish in Black-burnished ware. GE.44 with a fragment from the same context as nos. 424-431 below.

412.	Bowl or dish in a soft light buff fabric. CP.4.

413.	Bowl in a light grey sandy fabric with darker surfaces; cf. Gillam 1970, type 301 (A.D.80-130). CP.5.

414.	Tazza in a soft pinky-buff fabric. CP.1.

415.	Bowl or dish in a soft light-grey fabric. AD.1.

416.	Bowl in a soft buff fabric. Possibly a Wilderspool product. EO.2.

417.	Bowl in a soft buff fabric. Possibly a Wilderspool product. EO.3.

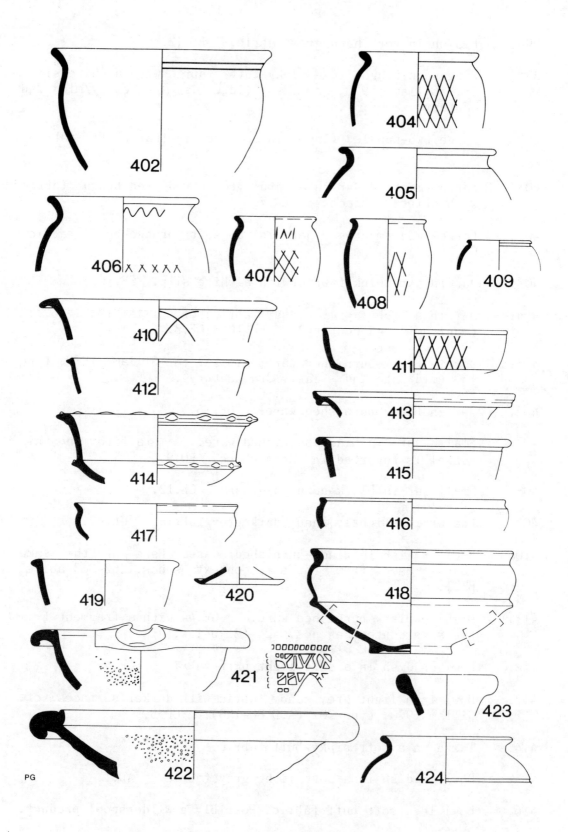

Fig.25. Coarse pottery nos. 402, 404–424. Scale 1:4.
Drawn by Paul Gibbons.

418.   Bowl in a soft dark pink fabric reminiscent of the samian form 44. The exterior bears red-brown paint. A Wilderspool product, cf. Hartley 1981, p.476, no.3. EO.1.

419.   Bowl or dish in Black-burnished ware. FR.6.

420.   Lid in a slightly sandy red-browm fabric. DS.1.

421.   Mortarium (Diameter 24cms.) in a fairly soft, fine-textured, orange-brown fabric with a thick grey core and traces of a very thin cream slip. There are quartz, red-brown sandstone and grey trituration grits and a small amount of tempering of the same type. The two-line stamp may be a trademark but it is possible to read AVST (in the top line with the lower line as some version of MANV); cf. Hartley & Webster 1973, Fig.8, N. There is growing evidence to suggest that Austinus began his working life at Wilderspool. This stamp also has characteristics in common with the trademark on no.584 below. Stamps from the same die are now known from Hardknott, Lancaster (3), Melandra Castle, Ribchester (4), Watercrook (2) and Wilderspool (3). The potter using this die, whether Austinus or not, undoubtedly worked at Wilderspool; the rim-forms associated are pre-Antonine and, if the links with Austinus are taken into consideration, a date within the period A.D. 120-140+ is likely for this die. (KFH) EQ.9. & EP.5.

422.   Mortarium in a hard close-bodied cream-coloured fabric with pink and grey grits. From below the cobbles. ER.1.

423.   Flagon in buff fabric. FR.4.

In addition the context yielded fragments of vessels nos. 376-7 above.

From Feature 11b (Section J-H, 8-10):
424.   Jar in a soft, slightly sandy grey fabric. J-H, 9. GJ.3.

425.   Narrow-mouthed jar in a very hard fabric with a grey core, brown margins and dark grey surfaces. J-H, 10. GM.13.

426.   Jar in Black-burnished ware; cf. Gillam 1970, type 122, (early - mid 2nd century). J-H, 10. GM.2.

427.   Jar in Black-burnished ware. J-H, 10. GM.16.

428.   Beaker in Black-burnished ware. J-H, 9. GJ.14.

429.   Bowl in pink fabric with dark grey surfaces. J-H, 9. GK.2.

430.   Thick-walled dish in hard pink fabric.   J-H, 9.   GK.13.

431.   Lid in soft slightly sandy grey fabric.   J-H, 9.   GK.10.

From J-H, 9 also came a dish similar to no. 351 above and a fragment of no. 411 above.

From the early road:
432.   Jar in Black-burnished ware.   DT.2.

433.   Flat-rimmed bowl in Black-burnished ware.   FV.7.

434.   Flat-rimmed bowl or dish in Black-burnished ware.   EM.1, with a further fragment from the same context as nos. 477-512 below.

435.   Dish in hard soapy grey fabric. FT.5.

436.   Bowl with an exagerated flange in a hard self-coloured pink fabric; similar to Gillam 1970, type 192 (early-mid 2nd century).   GG.3.

437.   Lid in grey fabric with a lighter core. Sherds of the same vessel come from the pebble path (feature 52).   FV.3.

Also from this context was a vessel similar to no.457 below.

From the late road:
438.   Flagon in hard white fabric.   CH.5.

439.   Flagon in fairly soft grey fabric.   BF.9.

440.   Flagon in an open-bodied cream fabric with a slightly darker slip.   BF.31.

441.   Narrow-mouthed jar in a soft orange fabric.   BF.29.

442.   Jar in Black-burnished ware; cf. Gillam 1976, no.30 (early-mid 2nd century). Part of this vessel comes from above the drainage channel, see nos. 546-565 above.   BF.20.

443.   Jar in light grey-cored orange fabric.   AO.6.

444.   Segmental bowl in a grey-cored fabric with pink margins; cf. Gillam 1970, type 294 (A.D. 120-150). Two examples. BF.19.

445.   Bowl in soft buff fabric.   BF.12.

446.   Bowl in soft dark pink fabric probably from Wilderspool. BF.30.

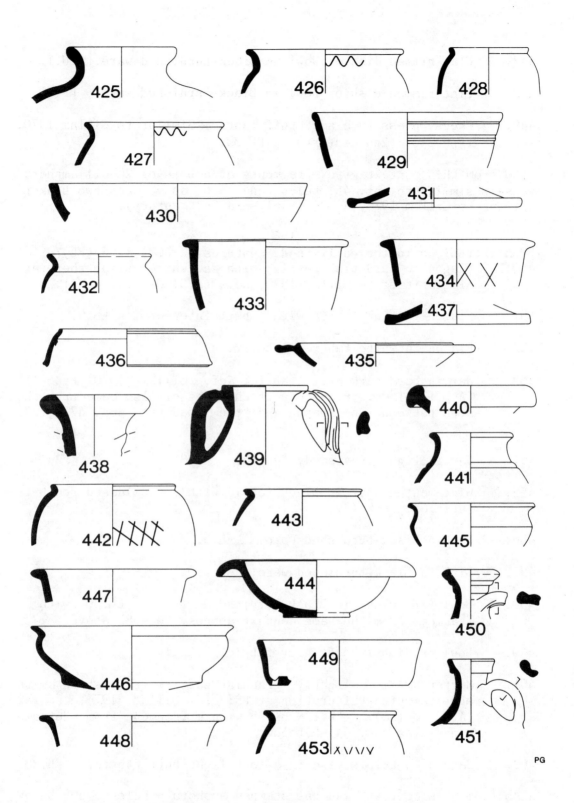

Fig.26. Coarse pottery nos. 425-453. Scale 1:4.
Drawn by Paul Gibbons.

447.   Flat-rimmed dish or bowl in Black-burnished ware. BU.1.

448.   Flat-rimmed dish or bowl in Black-burnished ware. BF.10.

449.   Cheese press in a soft buff fabric. Similar to Gillam 1970,
         type 350 (2nd century).   BF.33.

Also from this context were fragments of a Dressel 20 oil amphora,
vessels similar to nos. 451 below and 426 above and two beakers
similar to Gillam 1976, no.24 (early-mid 2nd century).

From intrusions in the early road, features 32 (CM) & 58 (EL):
450.   Flagon in hard pink fabric with a white slip; there are
         similarities to Gillam 1970, no.4 (A.D.90-130). CM.1.

451.   Flagon in pink fabric with a buff interior .   EL.9.

452.   Flagon in white fabric.   EL.12.

453.   Jar in hard dark grey fabric; cf. Gillam 1970, type 116
         (A.D.130-150). Fragments of this vessel also came from the
         area between the path and the road (see nos. 477-512).
         CM.2.

454.   Jar in light grey sandy fabric.   EL.8.

455.   Wide-mouthed jar in black fabric with an oxidised red-buff
         interior.   EL.13.

456.   Jar in Black-burnished ware.   EL.3.

457.   Dish in Black-burnished ware.   EL.10.

458.   Bowl or dish in Black-burnished ware.   EL.30 with a
         fragment from the same context as nos. 362-383 above.

459.   Bowl or dish in soft grey fabric.   EL.14.

461.   Mortarium in slightly granular soft white fabric with
         multicoloured triuration grits; cf. Gillam 1970, no.242
         (A.D. 90-130).   EL.1 & BI.25 with a fragment from the same
         context as nos. 541-5 below.

462.   Base of a triple vase in a soft light buff fabric.   EL.38.

Also from this context was the stamped amphora handle no.595 below
and vessels similar to nos.369 and 418 above and 507 below.

From an intrusion on the edge of the late road:
463.   Mortarium in hard pink fabric with orange surfaces and
         multicoloured trituration grits; cf. Hartley & Webster
         1973, no. 103. BE.2.

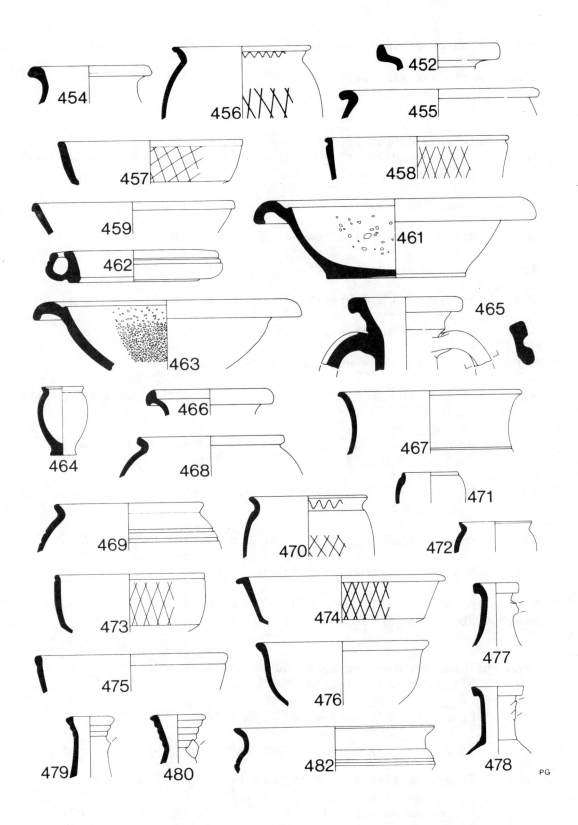

Fig.27. Coarse pottery nos. 454–480, 482. Scale 1:4.
Drawn by Paul Gibbons.

464.   Beaker or small jar in orange-pink fabric.   BE.13.

Also a mortarium similar to no. 382 above and a fragment of no.491
below.

From early road debris (Section G-F, 6):
465.   Double-handled flagon in hard cream fabric with pink
        surfaces.   DE.2.

466.   Flagon in a laminar white fabric.   FG.2.

467.   Wide mouthed jar in soft light grey soapy fabric.   DE.9.

468.   Jar in hard pinky-buff fabric.   DY.8.

469.   Jar in hard mid-grey fabric.   EI.1.

470.   Small jar in Black-burnished ware.   DY.10.

471.   Beaker in Black-burnished ware.   ES.3.

472.   Beaker in soft grey-brown fabric with slightly gritty
        surfaces.   EI.2.

473.   Bead rim bowl in Black-burnished ware; cf. Gillam 1976,
        no.52 (mid-late 2nd century).   DY.12.

474.   Dish in Black-burnished ware; cf. Gillam 1976, no.59 (mid
        2nd century).   FW.23.

475.   Bowl or dish in a hard close-bodied grey fabric.   ES.2.

476.   Bowl in soft buff-grey fabric.   DE.4.

Also a fragment of no. 486 and 523 below and vessels similar to
nos.549 above and 383 below.

From the area between the path and the road:
477.   Flagon in white fabric.   FB.15

478.   Flagon in soft grey-cored pink fabric.   CL.38.

479.   Ring-neck flagon in very hard grey fabric.   FF.16.

480.   Ring-neck flagon in soft buff fabric.   FF.15.

481.   Large narrow-necked jar in a sandy grey-brown fabric.
        BO.2.

482.   Bowl in a fairly soft close-bodied grey fabric.   FB.11.

483.   Jar in a grey-cored fabric with buff margins and grey interior.   FB.12.

484.   Jar in soft light grey fabric; cf. Gillam 1970, type 108 (A.D. 80-130).   CL.54.

485.   Jar in soft sandy grey fabric.   CL.21.

486.   Jar in soft sandy grey fabric. Part of this vessel comes from the early road see nos. 465-476 above.   CL.57.

487.   Narrow mouthed jar in a light grey gritty fabric with black surfaces.   CL.5.

488.   Rusticated jar in a smooth light grey fabric.   CL.49.

489.   Rusticated jar in gritty grey fabric.   EZ.9.

490.   Jar in soft grey fabric.   DU.9.

491.   Jar in Black-burnished ware. A fragment of this vessel comes from the intrusion in the late road (see nos.463-4 above). BO.3.

492.   Jar in Black-burnished ware.   DM.4.

493.   Carinated beaker in a fine dark grey fabric.   EU.3.

494.   Cornice-rim beaker in a buff fabric with purple-brown colour coating and roughcast surfaces. A North Gaulish product, cf. Anderson 1981, p.326 (late 1st to mid 2nd century).   CL.36.

495.   Flat-rimmed dish in Black-burnished ware; cf. Gillam 1976, no.60 (mid 2nd century).   CL.45.

496.   Dish in Black-burnished ware; despite the resemblance to Gillam 1976, no.73 (early 3rd century) the context would suggest a slightly earlier date.   CL.6.

497.   Bowl in soft orange fabric reminiscent of the samian form 37.   BO.13.

498.   Bowl in a soft light grey-brown fabric. Somewhat reminiscent of the samian form 37.   CL.2.

499.   Rusticated jar in a gritty grey fabric with black outer surfaces.   CL.59.

500.   Bowl or dish in soft buff fabric.   EU.11.

501.   Carinated flat-rimmed bowl in soft grey fabric.   EU.2.

502.   Flat-rim bowl in a slightly sandy soft grey fabric.   DU.12.

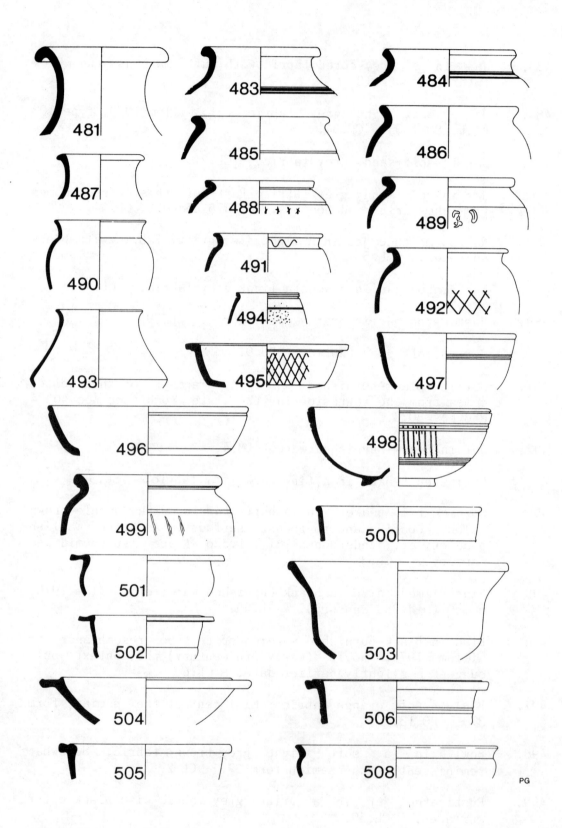

Fig.28. Coarse pottery nos. 481, 483–506, 508. Scale 1:4.
Drawn by Paul Gibbons.

503.   Carinated bowl in grey fabric.   FF.25.

504.   Flanged bowl or dish in soft light grey fabric.   FF.1.

505.   Reeded rim bowl or dish in soft light grey fabric.   CL.24.

506.   Reeded rim bowl in cream fabric; cf. Gillam 1970, type 215 (A.D. 80-125).   DU.7.

507.   Carinated bowl in soft pink-buff fabric.   DM.6.

508.   Bowl in soft orange-pink fabric; cf. Hartley & Webster 1973, nos.54-5.   DM.13.

509.   A large portion of a mortarium (diameter c. 31cms.) in hard fine-textured, creamy-buff fabric with a grey core and a little fine quartz and less red-brown tempering. The trituration grit is mainly quartz with a very few blackish grits. The stamp is from an unknown die and is too fragmentary to read. The mortarium was probably made in the Midlands c. A.D. 100-140.   (KFH)   DM.14.

510.   Mortarium in a very hard grey-cored orange fabric with white grits and traces of a cream slip on the interior; cf. Gillam 1970, type 245 (early-mid 2nd century).   DU.5.

511.   Bottle in a very hard grey fabric.   BO.22.

512.   Dish in soft pink fabric. Possibly a Wilderspool product (Hartley & Webster 1973, no.66).   CL.19.

Also the stamped Dressel 20 handle no.594 below and fragments of nos. 434 and 453 above.

512 A&B   Fragments of two mortaria in fairly fine-textured cream fabric with a darker slip; the fabric is tempered with a little quartz and with less red-brown material. The trituration grit is mainly quartz with some brown, one haematite and a few dark grey grits. The two-line stamps on these fragments are from the single die of Vitalis IV. The name appears on both lines of the stamp though there are a few slight differences notable in the L. One kiln used only by Vitalis and another which he may have shared with Minomelus and Gratinus have been excavated at Hartshill, Warks. Forty-two stamps of his are now known from England (excluding the kiln site) and one from Newstead in Scotland. The latter must be from the Antonine occupation; any association with Minomelus and Gratinus could well date to this period. However, his distribution pattern in general is a typical one for a pre-Antonine potter and many

of his rims have a clear affinity with those of G.Attius Marinus, one of the earliest mortarium potters to work at Mancetter and Hartshill. The evidence as a whole points to activity c.A.D. 115-145. The two mortaria from Ribchester are not characteristic of his earliest products. (KFH) DM.9 (no.512A) & BA.1 (no.512B).

From the pit, feature 60:
513.   Jar in slightly gritty grey fabric.   EY.1.

514.   Jar in soft bright orange fabric.   EY.9.

515.   Dish in Black-burnished ware; cf. Gillam 1976, no.73 (early 3rd century).   EY.3.

516.   Dish in Black-burnished ware.   EY.10.

From the path:
517.   Flagon in soft light grey fabric.   DP.6.

518.   Jar in soft orange-buff fabric.   DP.10.

519.   Flat-rimmed dish in Black-burnished ware;   cf. Gillam 1976, no.63 (mid - late 2nd century).   DP.3.

Also a fragment of the lid no.437.

From timber trenches to the South of the path, feature 47:
520.   Jar in soft light grey fabric with gritty surfaces.   DH.2.

521.   Jar in a soft soapy grey fabric.   DH.5.

522.   Beaker in pink fabric with roughcast exterior and brown colour coating. Cf. Anderson 1981, p.333;; Gillam 1970, type 72 (late 1st - mid 2nd century). A further fragment of this vessel comes from section C-D, 8, see no.527 below. EH.2.

523.   Lid in a slightly sandy yellow-buff fabric. A further fragment of this vessel came from the early road, see nos. 465-476 above.   CV.10.

524.   Lid in Black-burnished ware; cf. Holt, Grimes 1930, no. 100 (2nd century).   DH.11.

Also a jar, probably rusticated and similar to no. 488 above.

From the drainage channel:
525.   Small jar in hard grey sandy fabric. DB.2. From primary silt (Section C-D, 7).

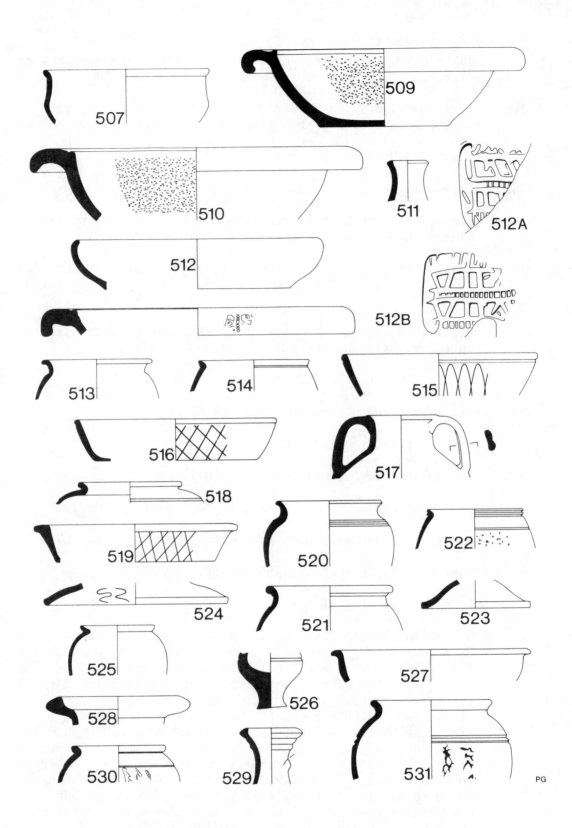

Fig.29. Coarse pottery nos. 507, 509-531.
Scale 1:4 (except stamps - 1:2).
Drawn by Paul Gibbons.

526.   Unguentarium in a hard white fabric. The base is somewhat distorted. FM.1. From the sump (section A-B, 15).

527.   Flat-rimmed dish in a fairly soft gritty light grey fabric. CN.10. From C-D, 8 with a fragment of beaker no. 522 above.

Nos.528-540 are from Section C-D, 5-6:

528.   Large flagon in hard sandy buff fabric.   CN.9.

529.   Flagon in pink-buff fabric; similar to Gillam 1970, type 4 (late 1st - early 2nd century).   CN.23.

530.   Rusticated jar in soft black fabric. There are similarities to Gillam 1970, type 98 (late 1st - early 2nd century). CN.18.

531.   Rusticated jar in a gritty black fabric with lighter surfaces, oxidised red-buff in places.   CN.32.

532.   Jar in hard brittle grey fabric.   CN.29.

533.   Jar in very hard grey fabric.   CN.4.

534.   Jar in slightly sandy black fabric.   CN.8.

535.   Jar in hard light buff fabric.   CN41.

536.   Wide-mouthed jar in a hard light grey fabric.   CN.19.

537.   Flanged bowl in very hard grey fabric; 2 examples.   CN.31.

538.   Bowl or dish in soft pink-buff fabric.   CN.46.

539.   Flanged dish in grey fabric.   CN.7.

540.   Mortarium. Flange fragment in fine-textured, softish, very pale grey fabric (intended to be cream) with quartz and a blackish tempering material. The fragmentary stamp is from one of the two dies reading QIVS CRES presumably for Q. Iustius Crescens. His stamps have now been noted from Aldborough, Catterick, Doncaster, Leicester, Old Winteringham (2), Ribchester (2) and Templeborough. The fabric and slip used by him strongly point to an origin in Lincolnshire and the distribution of his work is similar to that of Aesico who worked in North-West Lincolnshire. There is no site dating evidence for Crescens but his mortaria appear to be earlier than those of Aesico; they would best fit a date c. A.D. 100-140.   (KFH)   CN.11.

Also a lid similar to no. 561 below and two sherds with graffito (archive report).

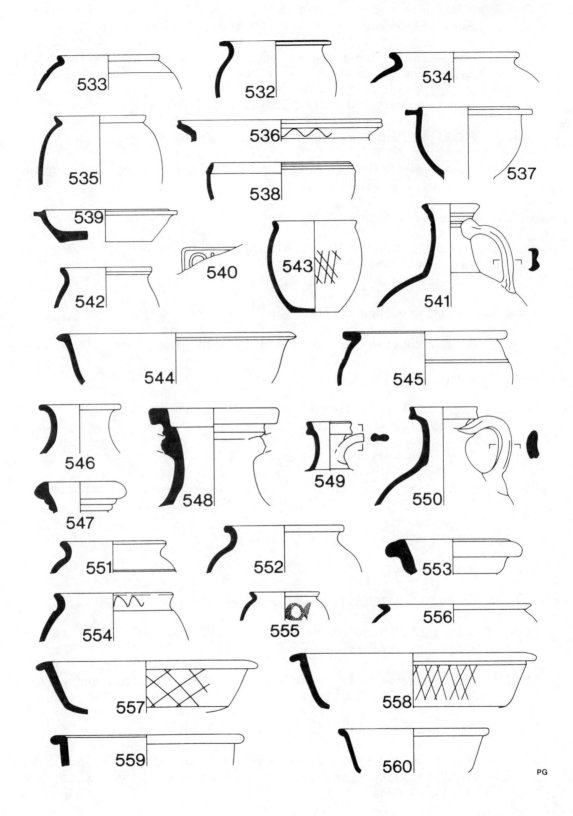

Fig.30. Coarse pottery nos. 532–561.
Scale 1:4 (except no.540 – 1:2)
Drawn by Paul Gibbons.

Nos. 541–545 are from section A–B, 9 and C–D, 2:

541.   Ring-neck flagon in orange-pink fabric; cf. Gillam 1970, types 2–4 (late 1st – early 2nd century).   FC.6.

542.   Jar in a very hard dark grey fabric.   ET.2.

543.   Small jar in Black-burnished ware.   BI.10.

544.   Flat-rimmed dish or bowl in soft grey slightly granular fabric.   BI.8.

545.   Wide-mouthed jar in soft buff fabric.   ET.1.

Also the stamped Dressel 20 handle, no.593 below and a fragment of the mortarium no. 461 above.

From above the drainage channel (Section E–A, 3–4):

546.   Narrow mouthed jar or flagon in hard pink fabric.   EK.1.

547.   Ring-neck flagon in a hard white fabric.   CB.2.

548.   Large double-handled flagon in hard orange-pink fabric with traces of a white slip.   AN.9.

549.   Flagon in soft buff fabric.   AN.5.

550.   Flagon in soft buff fabric; there are similarities to Gillam 1970, type 16 (A.D.170–240).   AN.8.

551.   Jar in grey sandy fabric.   DF.5.

552.   Jar in smooth soft grey fabric.   CB.1.

553.   Flagon in soft grey-cored pale orange fabric.   EA.1.

554.   Jar in Black-burnished ware; cf. Gillam 1976, no.1. (early – mid 2nd century).   DF.8.

555.   Beaker in a soft pink fabric with buff painted circle decoration.   CD.11.

556.   Jar in hard light buff fabric.   CD.10.

557.   Flat-rimmed dish in Black-burnished ware ; cf. Gillam 1976, no.62 (mid 2nd century). For a graffito on this vessel see archive. CI.4.

558.   Flat-rimmed dish in Black-burnished ware; cf. Gillam 1976, no.59 (mid 2nd century).   BD.1.

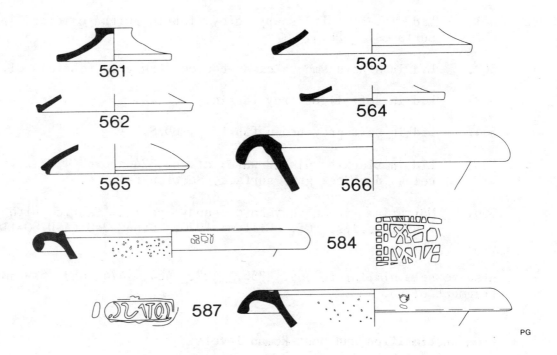

561

562

563

564

565

566

584

587

PG

Fig.31. Coarse pottery nos. 562-566, 584, 587.
Scale 1:4 (except stamps - 1:2).
Drawn by Paul Gibbons.

559.   Flat-rimmed bowl or dish in in soft slightly sandy grey
       fabric.   CD.8.

560.   Dish in soft slightly sandy orange fabric. BD.16 & CD.12.

561.   Lid in a soft soapy grey fabric with oxidised pink
       surfaces.   DF.4.

562.   Lid in a hard smooth close-bodied dark grey fabric. CI.7.

563.   Lid in soft light grey fabric.   CD.13.

564.   Lid in soft grey-brown fabric.   BD.8.

565.   Lid in Black-burnished ware; cf. no.524 above.   CX.2. From
       below daub/pea grit surface, Section E-A, 4.

566.   Mortarium in a very hard sandy yellow fabric with no
       visible grits. Cf. Gillam 1970, type 240 (A.D.80-110).
       DF.1.

Also vessels similar to nos. 356, 407, 464, 474 and 529 and a
fragment of no. 442.

From unstratified and post-Roman levels:

       A report upon **nos. 567-592** with illustrations will be
placed in the site archive.   Of these vessels only the stamped
mortaria nos. 584 and 587 are published here.

584.   Mortarium (diameter 30 cms.) in   soft   fine-textured,
       orange-brown fabric with a thick grey core with very fine
       quartz and red-brown tempering; a few quartz and grey
       trituration grits survive. It probably had a cream slip
       though no certain traces survive. The two-line trademark
       stamp is probably the work of an illiterate potter (Hartley
       & Webster 1973, Fig.8, 0), whose stamps are now known from
       Ambleside, Hardknott, Lancaster, Ravenglass, Ribchester and
       Watercrook. The fabric and forms used and the distribution
       are entirely typical for a Wilderspool potter. Mortaria
       were being produced at Wilderspool c. A.D. 100-165 and the
       rim-forms associated with the stamp point strongly to
       pre-Antonine activity. (KFH)   AA.56.

587.   Mortarium (diameter c.30 cms.) in fine-textured creamy
       white fabric with noticably less tempering than the Vitalis
       mortaria (nos. 512 A & B above); a few red-brown, quartz
       and dark grey trituration grits survive. The retrograde
       stamp is from one of at least seven dies used by Icotasgus
       who worked in the Mancetter-Hartshill   potteries   in
       Warwickshire. Five of his stamps have been recorded from
       Antonine deposits in Scotland and 54 from sites throughout
       England and Wales, excluding 13 from the kiln site at

Mancetter. Igotasgus has a fairly typical distribution for a Mancetter potter working in the Antonine period but some of his mortaria show pre-Antonine characteristics in the rim forms and the trituration grit used. A date of c.A.D. 130-160 would fit his work well.

Stamps on Amphorae. (JJP).

The handles considered here are all from examples of Dressel 20, the large spherical amphoare for oil from the Guadalquivir region in the Roman province of Baetica in Spain. These amphorae have a long history which runs from the first to the third century A.D. For details including the evolution of the shape, see Peacock & Williams 1986, pp. 136-140.

593.   Handle in a grey-pink clay with fine grit. The rather faint rectangular stamp probably reads LVC, perhaps a stamp of L. V[ibius] Ch[rom...], cf. Callender 1965, nos. 975 & 981. BI.19.

594.   Handle in grey-brown clay with fine grit. The faint rectangular stamp reads SLP . For a possible comparison see the stamp from Corbrdge apparently reading S.I.P., Callender 1949, 97; Callender 1965, no. 1627). BO.21.

595.   Handle with a right angled profile. The reading of the stamp is unclear but possibly reads A Q. Possibly ?M.Ant[onius] Q[....] or ?M. Anto[nius]. See also Callender 1965, no. 1018 (MAP); there is also some resemblance to ibid. no.1142a (MMR) from Ilkley (Woodward 1926, 258). EL.11.

Graffiti.

Reports on graffiti on both samian and coarse pottery will be placed in the site archive.

g) **The School Field, 1974.**
   By P.V.Webster.

As is the case with most other reports in this section, a slightly expanded version of the report on the School Field coarse pottery will be placed in the site archive. The catalogue below is arranged in approximately the same order as the structural report (Part 2, Chapter 7).

a) **Trench C.**

From a pit:

600.   Jar in Black-burnished ware; cf. Gillam 1976, no.10 (late 3rd century). C.9.

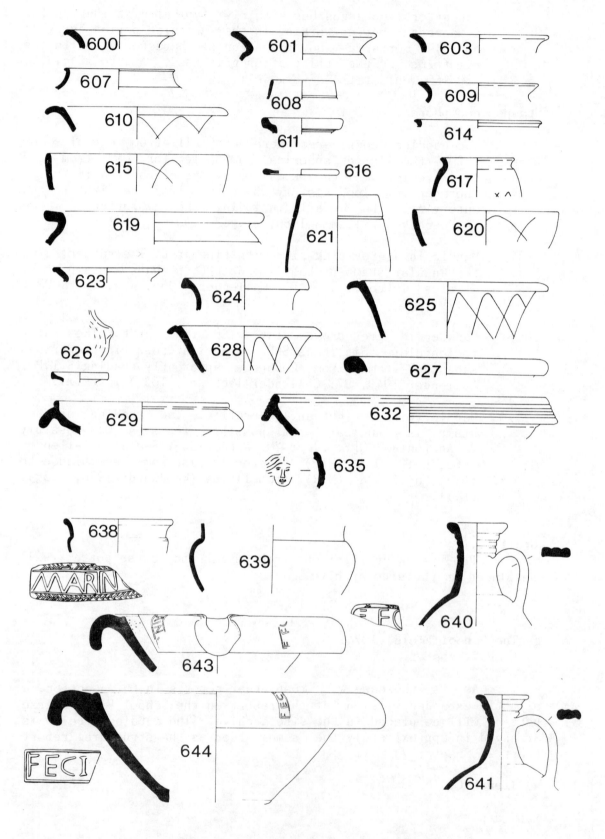

Fig.32. Coarse pottery nos. 600-641.
Scale 1:4 (except stamps - 1:2).

601.   Jar in Black-burnished ware; Gillam 1976, no.9 (mid – late 3rd century) is similar and probably of a similar date. C9 (with a further fragment from C.8).

602.   (Not illustrated). Jar in Black-burnished ware; cf. Gillan 1976, no.6 (early 3rd century). C.9.

603.   Jar in mid grey fabric. C.8.

604.   (Not illustrated). Wall fragment of a beaker in Nene Valley fabric, pale pinky white with a dark grey-brown colour coat; from a vessel similar to Gillam 1970, type 92 (A.D. 180–250). C.8.

605.   (Not illustrated). Fragments probably of two beakers in Nene Valley fabric as no. 604 above. One is a basal fragment from a large, comparatively coarse beaker and the other a wall fragment from a barbotine decorated beaker. Late 2nd – 3rd century. C.8.

606.   (Not illustrated). Two fragments of mortarium in Wilderspool fabric; cf. Hartley & Webster 1973, no.113 (early – mid 2nd century). C.8.

607.   Beaker in Nene Valley fabric, off white with a grey-brown colour coat; possibly similar to Gillam 1970, type 93 (A.D. 210–250). C.6.

608.   Beaker in Nene Valley fabric as no.607 above; cf. Gillam 1970, type 81 (A.D. 220–260).

609.   Jar in Black-burnished ware; cf. Gillam 1976, no.9 (mid – late 3rd century); with fragments from at least one other Black-burnished ware jar. C.6.

610.   Flanged and grooved bowl in Black-burnished ware; cf. Gillam 1976, no.42 (late 2nd – early 3rd century). The four other Black-burnished bowl fragments from this level are all from a single vessel chamfered at the base. Despite the rarity of chamfering on the type it is most likely that the basal and rim fragments belong to the same vessel (cf. Gillam 1976, pp. 68–70). C.6.

        Layer C.6 also yielded fragments of at least five other colour coated vessels, four probably of Nene Valley origin and one from Central Gaul. The overall date of the pit C.6/7/8 is clearly 3rd century. The latest piece appears to be no.600 (late 3rd century) from the lowest level but the majority of pieces are either early – mid or mid – late third century. Deposition in the middle or mid/late 3rd century seems most likely

From the levelling for the upper timber building:
611.   Flagon in orange fabric; cf. Milecastle 48 (Gibson &

Simpson 1911) pl.IV, 14 (Probably Hadrian's Wall Period II, 3rd century). C.5.

612. (Not illustrated). Small fragment of a 'Hunt cup' in off white fabric with a grey-brown colour coat; cf. Gillam 1970, types 84-5 & 89 (late 2nd - mid 3rd century). This type of vessel was produced both at Koln and in the Nene Valley (cf. Anderson 1981, pp. 325-331) but a Nene Valley origin seems more probable in view of the large amount of other probable Nene Valley products from this excavation. C.5.

613. (Not illustrated). Jar in Black-burnished ware similar to no. 609 above (mid - late 3rd century). C.5.

From the late timber building:

614. Rim of a beaker in off-white fabric with a red-brown colour coat. The rim is of the so-called 'cornice' type produced both by the Nene Valley and Koln potters (see no. 612 above). Cf. Gillam 1970, types 85-6, 88 (late 2nd - mid 3rd century). C.3.

615. Dish in Black-burnished ware; cf. Gillam 1976, no.77 (late 2nd - early 3rd century). C.3. (with a further fragment from C.2).

C.2. also produced a fragment of 'Castor Box'.

b) Trench A.

From levels prior to the Masonry building:

616. Amphora stopper in light buff fabric. Cf. Wroxeter (Atkinson 1942), p.288, A.14 with references. The use of these stoppers from an early date is attested by their appearance in the Neronian fortress at Usk (publication forthcoming) and in the Port Vendres II wreck (Colls et.al. 1977). Stoppers of this type are most likely to be associated with the globular Dressel 20 oil amphorae although use in other South Spanish amphorae is not unknown (ibid. pp.24, 34 & 38-40). In this case fragments of a Dressel 20 amphora come from the same level. A.6.

617. Jar in Black-burnished ware sooted externally. Typologically this is early in the North British series and a date in the Hadrianic or Hadrianic-Antonine period seems likely. A.6.

From the foundations of the masonry building:

618. (Not illustrated). Wall sherds of a jar in Black-burnished ware with very obtuse angled lattice and a faint horizontal line at the top of the decoration. Decoration of this type is unlikely to pre-date the late 3rd century. A.5.

619. Jar in coarse hard mid-grey fabric with a lighter partially oxidised core and sandy filler. A.4.

620. Dish in Black-burnished ware; Gillam 1976, no.18 (late 3rd century) has similarities. A.4.

From the disturbed demolition level of the masonry building:
621. Beaker in off-white fabric with a grey-brown colour coat; probably of Nene Valley origin, cf. Gillam 1970, type 81 (A.D. 220-260). A.2.

622. (Not illustrated). Wall sherd from a scale beaker in Nene Valley fabric, creamy white with a grey-brown colour coat; cf. Gillam 1970, types 53 & 93 (3rd or early 4th century). A.2.

623. Jar in Black-burnished ware. Probably from a vessel such as Gillam 1976, no.13 (early - mid 4th century). A.2.

No.623 is the latest piece from the demolition deposit.The heavily disturbed nature of the upper levels must, of course, be born in mind. Nevertheless, with construction of the building probably in the late third century, demolition in the early to mid fourth century is not improbable.

c) **Trench B.**

From the upper timber building debris:
624. Jar in soft smooth light orange-buff fabric; a product either of the Severn Valley or possibly of the Cheshire/Lancashire Plain although in the latter case the total lack of filler would be unusual. B.4.

625. Flanged and grooved bowl in Black-burnished ware; there is some similarity to Gillam 1976, no.42 (late 2nd - early 3rd century). B.4.

626. Neck fragment from a handled flagon in Nene Valley fabric, off white with a grey-brown colour coat. A small part of the handle survives together with a 'folded' projection to one side. Most probably this projection would have been matched by another on the other side of the handle. Such projections were common on bronze jugs (see for example, den Boersterd 1956, nos. 277-8 with references p.78; Tassinari 1975, nos. 171-6, 179). For a slightly cruder rendering of the same feature in a colour coated fabric (but not from the Nene Valley kilns) see Verulamium (Frere 1972) no. 1146. For comparable Nene Valley flagons cf. Great Casterton (Corder 1951, Fig.8, nos. 3-4; Corder 1961, Fig.24, no.11). B.2.

627.   Large jar in grey fabric. B.2.

628.   Flanged and grooved bowl in Black-burnished ware; cf.
        Gillam 1976, no.42 (late 2nd - early 3rd century). B.2.

629.   Mortarium in light red granula fabric, probably a
        Wilderspool product. B.2.

d) **Unstratified**.

        In the main, material from unstratified levels added little
to the general picture and have not been illustrated or listed.
Neither trenches D nor E penetrated stratified levels but both
produced some 3rd-4th century pieces from upper layers. A few,
mainly late pieces from trenches A-C are listed.

630.   (Not illustrated). Flanged and beaded bowl in
        Black-burnished ware; cf. Gillam 1976, no.46 (late 3rd -
        early 4th century). C+.

631.   (Not illustrated). Flanged and beaded bowl in abraded grey
        fabric probably of East Yorkshire origin and dating to the
        latter half of the fourth century. C+.

632.   Hammerhead mortarium in white fabric. Mancetter-Hartshill;
        cf. Gillam 1970, type 282 (A.D.230-340). B+.

633.   (Not illustrated). Wall sherd of a dimpled beaker in
        orange fabric with a dark brown 'metallic' colour coat.
        Probably a product of Central Gaul; cf. Greene 1978, Fig.
        2.3, no.5. Mid 2nd - mid 3rd century. C+.

634.   (Not illustrated). Wall sherd of a beaker in red and grey
        fabric with a dark grey 'metallic' colour coat; probably a
        product of the Rhine/Moselle region, cf. Greene 1978, Fig.
        2.3, no.6. Late 2nd - mid 3rd century. C+.

635.   Abraded face mask from a flagon in Nene Valley fabric, off
        white with traces of a light red-brown colour coat
        externally; cf. Hartley 1972, Fig.4, 15. The type appears
        in the destruction level of the Great Casterton Villa
        (Corder 1951, fig.8, 5) and its dating here is in general
        accord with that of the related Oxfordshire Ware type (cf.
        Young 1977, C11, pp. 148-150). See also an example from
        Carrawburgh (Wallis Budge 1903, p.68). Second half of 4th
        century. C+.

636.   (Not illustrated). Wall sherd of a beaker in Nene Valley
        fabric, off white with a grey-brown colour coat and
        barbotine decoration. The form is as Hartley 1960, Fig.4,
        6 but the decoration as ibid., Fig.4, 2. B+.

637.   (Not illustrated). Wall sherd of a beaker in Nene Valley

fabric, off white with a grey-brown colour coat. The
decoration is in the form of diagonal ridges. B+.

e) **General Discussion.**

The lowest levels of the School Field were not, of course,
sampled and the comparatively slight amount of late 1st and early
2nd century material need occasion little surprise. What pottery
there is of this date should be a pointer to early structures when
lower levels are excavated.

Much of the pottery covers the period between the late
second and early fourth centuries with late 2nd and early – mid 3rd
century pottery predominating in the material used for the
foundations of the late 3rd – 4th century masonry building. One
would expect, therefore, to see a number of colour coated vessels
represented but, even so, the number present seems unusually high.
In an effort to quantitfy this more closely and to identify the
relative importance of sources, a count of the minimum number of
vessels present in each layer was made. This detailed breakdown
will be deposited in the archive but the totals for the whole site
seem worthy of publication:

Vessel & Source	Minimum number of vessels	% of total
S.Spanish amphorae	11	7
BB1	27	18
Severn Valley Ware	2	1
Derbyshire Ware	1	1
Mortaria (all sources)	16	10
Colour coats:		
Lezoux	3	2
Rhine/Moselle	3	2
Oxfordshire	1	1
Nene Valley	27	18
Other (mainly local)	61	40
Total	152	100

Thus almost a quarter (23%) of all vessels, other than
samian, were colour coated finewares, mainly beakers. This seems a
very high percentage when compared with the amount of
Black-burnished ware (18%) and is in contrast to the situation on
the Access Road site (section g above) where only 6% of the pottery
was colour coated but 27% Black-burnished ware. We may also compare
the figures with those for the Great Casterton Barn destruction and
the well known Corbridge Destruction Deposit (Corder 1951, p.25)
which although they do not show sources show a very low percentage
of fine tableware (only 4% of the Great Casterton Deposit were
beakers and only 8% of the Corbridge deposit). Obviously only

further excavation, when it comes, will enable us to see whether it is really valid to draw any firm conclusions from the comparatively small sample gained in 1974. Meanwhile we may tentatively suggest that the unusually high number of fineware drinking vessels may be a product of the function of the building or of its social status. One wonders if this could for instance be the position of the mansio. Clearly only further work will tell but meanwhile the ceramic evidence from this site does stand out among the more mundane products of other civil sites at Ribchester,

h) **The Primary School Foundations**
By R.C.Turner & J.H.S.Witherington.

Possible Iron Age pottery:
638.   Jar in soft light grey fabric with a darker exterior and two narrow grooves on the shoulder.

639.   Wheel-made jar in a grey-cored red-brown fabric with a dark grey exterior.

Flagons:
    The large number of sherds in this class can be divided into three fabrics: white, pink and orange-buff. The latter, often with a cream slip was almost certainly made at Wilderspool.

640.   Orange buff fabric with traces of a cream slip. Similar to Gillam 1970, type 2 (A.D. 70-110).

641.   Fabric as no. 640 above. Similar to Gillam 1970, type 4 (A.D. 90-130).

642.   Coarse orange fabric with white translucent grits.

Mortaria:
643.   About three-quarters of the upper half of a well-worn mortarium (diameter c.28 cms.) in a granular greyish cream fabric with thick pink core and buff slip. The flint, quartz and red-brown trituration grits are combined with concentric scoring. The stamps read MARINVS //FECIT when complete. There are three dies which give the unequivocal reading MARINVS and at least four others including no. 644 below which are almost certainly to be attributed to him. See no. 644 below. (KFH) 161.270.

644.   One piece making just under a quarter of a worn mortarium (diameter c.40 cms) in a granular drab greyish cream fabric with a pale buff slip fired to brownish buff near the spout and on the outside. The clay has been tempered with fine

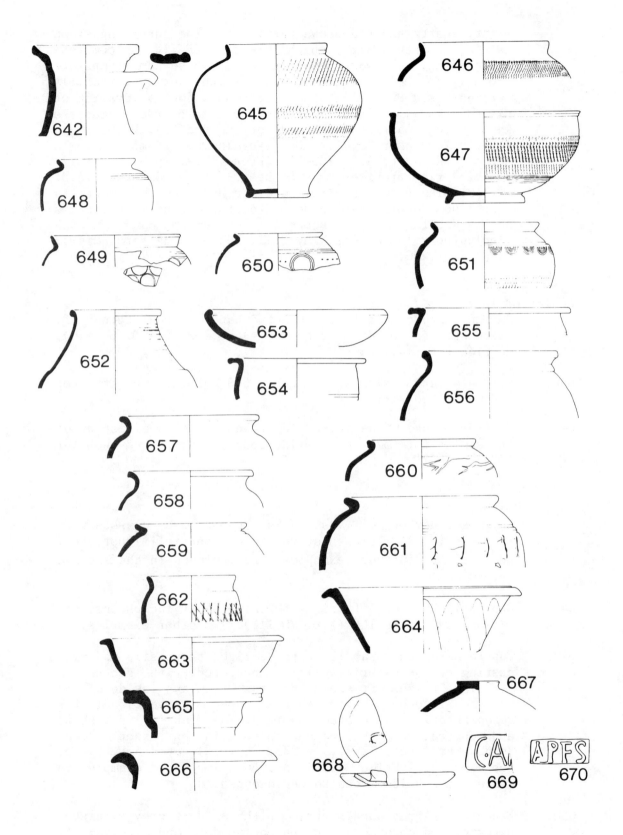

Fig.33. Coarse pottery nos. 642-670. Scale 1:4.

flint, quartz and red-brown particles. The surviving stamp is a counterstamp which reads FECIT in complete impressions. It was used by a potter whose namestamps are probably to be interpreted as Marinus or just possibly Martinus (see Bushe-Fox 1926, p.87, no.3 for a drawing of his namestamp). His stamps from the same pair of dies are known from Castleshaw, Doncaster, London (5), Richborough (2) and Verulamium (3). One Verulamium stamp is from a deposit dated to A.D. 105-115 (Frere 1972, p.376, no.27) and his rim profiles would best fit a date of c.A.D. 70-110. The forms, fabric and distribution of his mortaria leave no doubt that he worked on the extensive potteries near Watling Street between Verulamium and London (including kilns at Brockley Hill, Radlett and Verulamium). (KFH) 161.260.

Rouletted forms:

645.   Jar in hard orange fabric wth two bands of rouletting; cf. Manchester (Jones & Grealey 1974) no.152 (c.A.D. 80-140). Section E-F, 14.

646.   Jar in a fabric similar to no. 645 above, but thicker bodied with a grey core.

647.   Bowl in hard fine light red-brown fabric. Reminiscent of the samian form 37; cf. Wilderspool (Hartley & Webster 1973) no. 57.

Cups & Beakers:

A large number of vessels of these two classes were recovered. A representative selection is illustrated. Details of further examples are included in the archive report.

648.   Cup in light orange fabric with white sandy inclusions; cf. Gillam 1970, type 166 (A.D. 70-110). Two other examples.

649.   Cup in hard cream fabric with a light brown slip and mica dusting on the exterior. It is decorated with groups of circular bosses pressed outwards from the inside of the pot. Although many sherds are present, little reconstruction has proved possible. The fabric, rim shape and decorative technique can be seen in an example from Verulamium (Frere 1972, p.275, no.128) dated A.D. 60-75. See also Holt (Grimes 1930) no. 50. Two other examples in different fabrics are also represented.

650.   Beaker in a grey sandy fabric with a dark grey burnished exterior, decorated with barbotine dots and circles; cf. Gillam 1970, type 68 (A.D. 80-130).

651.   Beaker or small jar in a poor light grey sandy fabric with

burnished black exterior decorated in a 'pseudo-samian' style. A line of semi-circular 'ovolos' are stamped (rather than inscribed as in London Ware examples) and the body is covered with a rouletted design.

652.   Cup in a hard grey fabric with a lustrous interior and thin lines of burnishing arond the neck. Probably late 1st - early 2nd century.

Bowls & Dishes:
653.   Dish in a light grey fabric with coarse black sandy inclusions; cf. Gillam 1970, type 337, (A.D. 70-100) With one other example in coarse red fabric.

654.   Reed-rim bowl in soft light grey fabric with darker interior surface; cf. Gillam 1970, type 214 (A.D. 80-125).

655.   Reed-rim bowl in hard grey fabric with darker surfaces. Probably of similar date to no. 654 above.

Self-coloured & rusticated jars:
        These form the largest number of vessels with 28 different rims present. The plain vessels were made, almost exclusively, in a soft light grey fabric with a blotchy darker exterior. The rusticated jars form two main fabric groups, one in hard mid grey and the other (including most of the smaller vessels) in a lustrous grey fabric. Exceptions are the plain jar no. 657 and a rusticated body sherd (not illustrated) in an orange-buff fabric.

656.   Jar in soft light grey fabric with a darker exterior.

657.   Jar in hard orange-buff fabric with a burnished exterior.

658.   Jar in hard light grey sandy fabric with a darker exterior; cf. Gillam 1970, type 103 (A.D. 80-130).

659.   Jar or beaker in hard light grey fabric with a lustrous surface; cf. Gillam 1970, type 102 (A.D. 80-130).

660.   Jar in hard grey fabric with rusticated decoration trailed in horizontal lines; cf. Gillam 1970, type 97 (A.D. 80-130).

661.   Jar in coarse light grey sandy fabric with rusticated decoration; cf. Gillam 1970, type 95 (A.D.70-110).

Black-burnished ware (BB1):
662.   Small jar; cf. Gillam 1970, type 116 (A.D. 125-150).

663.   Dish; cf. Gillam 1970, type 309 (A.D.160-200).

664.   Bowl; cf. Gillam 1970, type 226 (A.D.220-270).

Other jars:
665.   Narrow-mouthed jar in orange fabric.

666.   Hook rim jar in a slightly micaceous orange fabric with a
          red core; cf. Wilderspool (Hartley & Webster 1973) no.10 &
          Gillam 1970, type 30. Perhaps mid 2nd century.

Lids:
          Twelve examples were found falling into two classes. An
          example of each is illustrated:

667.   Grey fabric; cf. Gillam 1970, type 340 (A.D.100-140).

668.   Soft orange fabric, having an inverted dome shape with a
          large pinch of clay taken just off centre. There are
          similarities to amphora stoppers (cf. no.616 above).

Stamped amphora handles:
669.   Fragment of a Dressel 20 handle in grey/pale brown fabric
          with fine grits. The beginning of the broken stamp reads
          C.A which is perhaps a stamp of G.Antonius Quietus, whose
          amphorae belong to the period c.A.D. 70-120 (Callender
          1965, p.90, no.243). ZQ.1.

670.   Curved Dressel 20 handle in pale pink/cream fabric with
          fine grits. The stamp is rectangular, 35 x 13 mm and reads
          APFS. See CIL 15.3069, 13.383 and Callender 1965, p.17,
          no.100b. The example from Rome was found on the eastern
          side of the Monte Testaccio which may suggest a date in the
          first half od the second century (Almeida 1972, p.113).
          ZA.1.

Chapter 3
ROMAN COINS FROM VICUS EXCAVATIONS
By D.C.A.Shotter

a) **Playing Fields, 1968–9.**

Original identification of coins from this excavation were by
J.P.C.Kent.

i) 1968 trial slot:
  Two coins were found, both of Vespasian's reign.

671.   AE   **dupondius**   A.D. 77–8.
        Obv.   T CAES IMP AVG F TR P COSVI CENSOR
        Rev.   FELICITAS PVBLICA S C

                                                        Lugdunum
                                                        RIC 775b.

672.   AE   **as** ·   A.D. 69–79.
        Obv.   IMP CAESAR VESPASIAN AVG [
        REV.   Illegible

ii) 1969 excavation:
  Five coins were found.

673.   AE   **as**   Vespasian   Illegible   A.D. 69–79.

674.   AE   **as**   Domitian   A.D.86
        Obv.   IMP CAES DOMIT AVG GERM COSXII CENS PER P P
        Rev   MONETA AVGVSTI S C
        Trench 1.101   **RIC** 335.

675.   AE   **as**   Domitian   Illegible   A.D. 81–96.

676.   AE   **sestertius**   Trajan   A.D. 103–111
        Obv.
        IMP CAES NERVAE TRAIANO AVG GER DAC P M TR P COSV P P
        Rev.   S P Q R OPTIMO PRINCIPI S C
        Hearth 1 (Trench 1.17)   **RIC** pp. 277 ff.

677.   AE   **dupondius**   Trajan   prob. A.D. 114–7.
        Obv.   Illegible; head, radiate, right
        Rev.   Providentia standing left?

                                                        RIC 665?

b) **The Sewerage Scheme, 1976.**

Five Roman coins were recovered:

678.   AE   **dupondius**   Trajan   A.D. 107.
        Obv.
        IMP CAES NERVAE TRAIANO AVG GER DAC [PM TRP] COSV P P
        Rev.   S P Q R OPTIMO PRINCIPI S C
        Moderate wear   **RIC** 48; Hill 316
        SF.4 (Cutting III, FN 345).

679.   AE   **as**   Vespasian   A.D. 69-79.
        Very worn and corroded
        SF.65 (Cutting I extension, unstratified).

680.   AE   **as**   Vespasian   A.D. 72-3.
        Obv.   IMP CAES VESPASIAN AVG COSIIII
        Rev.   PROVIDENT S C
        Moderate wear   **RIC** 746
        SF.74 (Cutting II, FN 235).

681.   AE   **dupondius**   Vespasian   A.D. 72-3.
        Obv.   ]COSIIII
        Rev.   Illegible
        Very corroded
        SF.76 (Cutting II, FN.214 = part of FN.228).

682.   AE   **sestertius**   Hadrian   A.D. 117-138.
        Obv.   IMP CAES TRAIANVS HADRIANVS AVG
        Rev.   Illegible
        Very worn
        SF.84 (Cutting III, FN.300).

c) **The Sheltered Housing Scheme, 1980.**

Two coins were found:

683.   AR   **denarius**   L.Aelius   A.D. 137.
        Obv.   L AELIVS CAESAR
        Rev.   TR POT COSII SALVUS
        Little wear   Hill 861
        SF.33 (RIB.80.005).

684.   AE   Radiate copy?   c.A.D. 270?
        Illegible fragment, probably from a silver washed radiate.
        SF.68 (RIB.80.030).

d) **The Access Road, 1977.**

Sixteen Roman coins were found:

685. AE   **as**   Vespasian   A.D.71?
      Obv.   Illegible
      Rev.   [PAX AVGVSTI S C]?
      Fragmentary but not very worn   **RIC** 493?
      SF.114.EU (from the area between the path and the road).

686. AE   **as**   Vespasian   A.D. 69-79.
      Illegible and very worn
      SF.47.BI (from the drainage channel, section C-D, 2).

687. AE   **as**   Domitian   A.D.83-96.
      Obv.   IMP CAES DOMIT AVG GERM [
      Rev.   Illegible
      SF.132.GM (from feature 11b, section J-H, 10).

688. AE   **as**   Domitian
      Illegible and very worn
      SF.20.AR (Unstratified).

689. AE   **sestertius**   Trajan   A.D. 103-111.
      Obv.
      IMP CAES NERVAE TRAIANO AVG GER DAC P M TR P COSV P P
      Rev.   (Abuntantia) S P Q R OPTIMO PRINCIPI S C
      Slightly worn   **RIC** 492
      SF.17.AA (Unstratified).

690. AE   **dupondius**   Trajan   A.D. 103-111.
      Obv.
      IMP CAES NERVAE TRAIANO AVG GER DAC P M TR P COSV P P
      Rev.   S P Q R OPTIMO PRINCIPI S C
      Worn   Possibly **RIC** 569-89
      SF.73.DE (from the early road debris, section G-F, 6).

691. AE   **sestertius**   Trajan   A.D. 103-111.
      Obv.
      IMP CAES NERVAE TRAIANO AVG GER DAC P M TR P COSV P P
      Rev.   S P Q R OPTIMO PRINCIPI S C
      Worn   Possibly **RIC** 547
      SF.103.EP (from the cobbled area, North-East corner of the
      site).

692. AE   **dupondius**   Trajan
      Illegible and very worn
      SF.32.BJ (from the yellow clay, section E-A, 4).

693. AE   **sestertius**   Trajan.
      Illegible and very worn
      SF.112.EB (from the stone building, section P-Q, 2).

694.   AE   **dupondius**   Hadrian   A.D. 123.
       Obv.   IMP CAESAR TRAIANVS HADRIANVS AVG P M TR P COSIII
       Rev.   VIRTVTI AVGVSTI S C
       Worn   **RIC** 605; Hill 250
       SF.65.AU (Unstratified).

695.   AE   **dupondius**   Hadrian   A.D. 132-4.
       Obv.   HADRIANVS AVGVSTVS
       Rev.   CLEMENTIA AVG COSIII P P S C
       Moderately worn   **RIC** 714
       SF.84.AA (Unstratified).

696.   AR   **denarius**   Hadrian   A.D. 132-4.
       Obv.   HADRIANVS AVGVSTVS
       Rev.   IVSTITIA AVG P P COSIII
       Slightly worn   **RIC** 215
       SF.95.ES (early road debris).

697.   AR   **denarius**   Hadrian   A.D. 134-8.
       Obv.   HADRIANVS AVG COSIII P P
       Rev.   FORTUNAE REDVCI
       Worn   **RIC** 248
       SF.24.AU (Unstratified).

698.   AR   **denarius**   Antoninus Pius A.D. 151-2.
       Obv.   ANTONINVS AVG PIVS P P TR P XV
       Rev.   (Annona standing left) COSIIII
       Fresh   **RIC** 204
       SF.102.ER (from the cobbled area, close to the North- East
       corner of the stone building).

699.   AE   **sestertius**   Antoninus Pius A.D. 138-161.
       Obv.   ANTONINVS AVG PIVS P P COS
       Rev.   (Abuntantia?)
       Moderately worn
       SF.13.AA (Unstratified).

700.   AE   **as**   Marcus Aurelius   A.D. 161-176.
       Obv.   FAVSTINA AVGVSTA
       Rev.   IVNO S C
       Fresh   **RIC** 1647
       SF.4.AA (Unstratified).

       There was in addition an illegible and very worn AE
       fragment (SF.104.EB) from the stone building.

e) **The School Field, 1974.**

       One coin was found (unstratified):

701.   AE   Constantinian   A.D. 330-341.
       Obv.   VRBS ROMA
       Rev.   She-wolf and twins (mm. illegible)

f) **The School foundations, 1977.**

One coin was found:

702. AE **dupondius**   Trajan   A.D. 116.
Obv.   IMP CAES NER TRAIANO OPTIMO AVG GER
          DAC PARTHICO P M TR P COSVI P P
Rev.   PROVIDENTIA AVGVSTI S P Q R S C
Little wear   **RIC** 664; Hill 732
Unstratified.

g) **Summary of unpublished coins found in the village in recent years.**

	Description	Location	Found	**RIC**
AE	**as** Vespasian	Outside White Bull Inn	1977	?
AE	**as** Vespasian	Rectory garden	1973	?
AE	**as** Domitian	Church Street	1968	?
AE	**sestertius** Trajan	White Bull Inn	1975	?
AE	**dupondius** Trajan	?	?	?
AR	**denarius** Hadrian	?	1967	309
AE	**as** Hadrian	White Bull Inn	1977	?
AE	**as** Sabina	Playing Field	1968	1023
AE	Radiate Tetricus I	Museum Cottage	1973	141
AE	**sestertius** Domitian	Transport Yard	1967	?
AR	**denarius** Domitian	Water Street	1967	154

In addition, the following thirteen unstratified coins were recovered in the period 1970–77 from the area of the **fort granaries:**

AE	**as** Nero		198
AR	**denarius** Trajan		98
AE	**sestertius** Trajan		?
AE	**dupondius** M.Aurelius	(Antoninus)	1305
AR	**denarius** Caracalla (?)		?
AE	Radiate Tetricus I		?

		LRBC
AE	Constantine I (GLORIA EXERCITVS)	1.49
AE	Constantine I (GLORIA EXERCITVS)	?
AE	Constantine I (she-wolf & twins)	1.51
AE	Constantine I (Victory on prow)	?
AE	Constantine I (GLORIA EXERCITVS)	1.88
AE	Constantine I (VRBS ROMA?)	?
AE	Constans (VICTORIAE D D AVGG Q N N)	1.148

BIBLIOGRAPHY AND ABBREVIATIONS

Almeida E.R. 1972   'Novedades de epigraphia anforaria del Monte Testaccio', **Recherches sur les amphores romaines**, Collection de l'ecole francaise de Rome, 113 ff.

Anderson A.C. 1981   'Some continental beakers of the first and second centuries A.D.' pp. 321-48 in Anderson A.C. & A.S. 1981.

Anderson A.C. & A.S. 1981   **Roman pottery research in Britain and North-West Europe**, BAR, Internat. Ser. 123, Oxford.

Atkinson D. 1914   'A hoard of samian ware from Pompeii', **J. Roman Studies**, 4, pp.27-64, pl.II-XVI.

Atkinson D. 1942   **Report on excavations at Wroxeter ... 1923-1927**, Birmingham.

Birley E.& M. 1938   'Fourth report on excavations at Chesterholm - Vindolanda', **Archaeologia Aeliana**, 4th ser., 15, 222-237.

Birley E. 1947   'The samian ware', pp. 98-108 in F.G.Simpson, K.S.Hodgson, 'The coastal mile-fortlet at Cardurnock', **Trans.Cumb.& Westmorland Ant. & Arch. Soc. N.S.**, 47, 78-127.

Bushe-Fox J.P. 1926   **First report on the excavations of the Roman fort at Richborough, Kent**, Report of Res. Comm. of Soc. of Ant. of London, no. 6.

Callender M.H. 1949   'Corbridge amphora stamps', **Archaeologia Aeliana**, 4th ser. 27, 60-124.

Callender M.H. 1965   **Roman amphorae**, Durham.

Colls D. et.al. 1977   **L'épave Port-Vendres II et le commerce de la Bétique a l'époque de Claude**, Archaeonautica I, CNRS, Paris.

Corder P. 1937   'A pair of fourth century Romano-British pottery kilns near Crambeck', **Ant.J.**, 17, 392-413.

Corder P. 1951   **The Roman town and villa at Great Casterton Rutland**, Nottingham.

Corder P. 1961   **The Roman town and villa at Great Casterton, Rutland, Third report..,** Nottingham

Crawford M.H. 1974   **Roman Republican coinage,** Cambridge.

Curle J. 1911.   **A Roman frontier post and its people. The Fort of Newstead in the parish of Melrose ,** Glasgow.

D.   see Déchelette 1904.

Dannell G.B. 1971   'The samian pottery', pp.260–316 in B. Cunliffe, **Excavations at Fishbourne, 1961–1969. Vol.II: The finds,** Report of Res. Comm. of Soc. of Ant. of London, no. 27.

Déchelette J. 1904   **Les vases céramiques ornés de la Gaule Romaine,** Vol.2, Paris.

den Boesterd M. 1956   **The bronze vessels in the Rijksmuseum G.M. Kam at Nijmegen,** Nijmegen.

Dodd P.W. & Woodward A.M. 1922   'Excavations at Slack, 1913–15', **Yorks Arch J.,** 26, 1–92.

Edwards B.J.N. & Webster P.V. 1985   **Ribchester Excavations. Part 1. Excavations within the Roman Fort, 1970–1980.** Cardiff.

Forster R.H. & Knowles W.H. 1911   'Corstopitum: report on the excavations in 1911', **Archaeologia Aeliana,** 3rd ser. 8, 137–263.

Frere S.S. 1972.   **Verulamium Excavations. Vol.1.** Report of Res.Comm. of Soc. of Ant. of London, no.28, 1972.

Gillam J.P. 1970.   **Types of Roman coarse pottery vessels in northern Britain,** 3rd Edition, Newcastle.

Gillam J.P.1976.   'Coarse fumed ware in North Britain and beyond', **Glasgow Arch.J.,** 4, 57–80.

Greene K.T. 1978   'Imported fine wares in Britain to A.D.250: a guide to identification', pp. 15–30 in P. Arthur, G. Marsh (Eds), **Early fine wares in Roman Britain,** BAR, British Ser., 57, Oxford.

Grimes W.H. 1930   **Holt, Denbighshire,** Y Cymmrodor, 41, London.

Hartley B.R. 1960   **Notes on the Roman pottery industry in the Nene Valley**, Peterborough Museum Soc. Occ. Papers 2 (reprinted 1972).

Hartley B.R. 1961   'Samian' in G.Webster, 'An excavation on the Roman site at Little Chester, Derby', **Derbys Arch.J.**, 81, 85-110.

Hartley B.R. 1972a   'The samian ware', pp.216-262 in Frere 1972.

Hartley B.R. 1972b   'The Roman occupation of Scotland: the evidence of samian ware', **Britannia**, 3, 1-55.

Hartley K.F. 1981   'Painted fine wares made in the Raetian workshops near Wilderspool, Cheshire', pp. 471-9 in Anderson A.C. & A.S. 1981.

Hartley K.F. & Webster P.V. 1973   'The Romano-British pottery kilns near Wilderspool', **Arch.J.**, 130, 77-103.

Hawkes C.F.C. 1927   'Excavations at Alchester, 1926', **Ant.J.**, 7, 155-184.

Hawkes C.F.C. & Hull M.R. 1947   **Camulodunum**, Report of Res. Comm. of Soc. of Ant. of London, no.14.

Hermet F. 1934   **La Graufesenque (Condatomago)**, Paris.

Hill P.V. 1970   **The dating and arrangement of the undated coins of Rome, A.D. 98-148**, London.

Hill P., Carson R., & Kent J. 1960   **Late Roman bronze coinage**, London.

Hinchcliffe J. & Williams J.H.   Report on excavations at Wilderspool 1965-1976 (forthcoming).

Howe M., Perrin J.R., & Mackreth D. 1980   **Roman pottery from the Nene Valley: a guide**, Peterborough.

Hull M.R. 1932   'The pottery from the Roman signal stations on the Yorkshire coast', **Arch J.**, 89, 220-253.

Hull M.R. 1963   **Roman pottery kilns of Colchester**, Report of Res. Comm. of Soc. of Ant. of London, no.21.

Jacobs J. 1912   'Sigillatafunde aus einen römischen Keller zu Bregenz', **Jahrbuch fur Altertumskund**, 6, 172-184 & Taf. I-V.

Jones G.D.B.   **Roman Manchester**, Manchester.
& Grealey S. 1974

Karnitsch P. 1959   **Die Reliefsigillata von Ovilava**, Linz.

Knorr R. 1919.   **Töpfer und Fabriken verzietter Terra-Sigillata des ersten Jahrhunderts**, Stuttgart.

Knorr R. 1952.   **Terra–Sigillata–Gefässe des ersten Jahrhunderts mit Töpfernamen**, Stuttgart.

LRBC   See Hill, Carson & Kent 1960.

Mattingley H.,   **Roman imperial coinage**, London.
Sydenham E.
& Sutherland C. 1923–83

Miller S.N. 1928   **The Roman fort at Old Kilpatrick**, Glasgow.

O.   See Oswald 1936–7.

O&P   See Oswald & Pryce 1920.

Oswald F.1936–7   **Index of Figure–Types on Terra–Sigillata**, Liverpool.

Oswald F. 1948   **The Terra Sigillata (samian ware) of Margidunum**, Nottingham.

Oswald F.   **Terra Sigillata**, London.
& Pryce F.D. 1920

Peacock D.P.S.   **Amphorae and the Roman economy**, London.
& Williams D.F. 1986

RIC   See Mattingley, Sydenham & Sutherland 1923–83.

Richmond I.A.   'Excavations on Hadrian's Wall in the Birdoswald–Pike Hill sector, 1929', **C&W**, 30, 169–205.
& Birley E. 1930

Richmond I.A.   'Excavations on the Roman site at Corbridge', **Archaeologia Aeliana**, 4th ser. 28, 152–201.
& Gillam J.P. 1950

Ricken H. 1934   'Die Bilderschüsseln der Kastelle Saalburg und Zugmantel', **Saalburg Jahrbuch**, 8, 130– 182.

Ricken H. 1948   **Die Bilderschüsseln der römischen Töpfer von Rheinzabern** (Tafelband), 2nd ed. Speyer.

Ricken H. & Fischer C. 1963   **Die Bilderschüsseln der römischen Töpfer von Rheinzabern** (Textband), Bonn.

Rogers   See Rogers 1974

Rogers G.B. 1974   **Poteries sigillées de la Gaule Centrale. I. Les motifs non figurés**, Gallia suppl. 8, Paris.

Rogers G.B. & Laing L.R. 1966   **Gallo-Roman pottery from Southampton**, Southampton.

S&S   See Stanfield & Simpson 1958.

Schonberger H. 1969   'The Roman frontier in Germany: an archaeological survey', **J.Roman Studies**, 59, 144-197.

Shaw R.C. 1926   'Excavations at Willowford', **Trans.Cumb.& Westmorland Ant. & Arch. Soc.**, 26, 429-506.

Stanfield J.A. & Simpson G. 1958   **Central Gaulish potters**, Durham.

Tassinari S. 1975   **La vaiselle de bronze, Romaine et Provinciale au Musée des Antiquités Nationales**, Gallia suppl. 29, Paris.

Terrisse J.R. 1968   **Les céramiques sigillées gallo-romaines des Martres-de-Veyre**, Gallia suppl. 19, Paris.

Thompson F.H. 1958   'A Romano-British pottery kiln at North Hykeham, Lincolnshire', **Ant.J.**, 38, 15-51.

Walke N. 1965   **Das römische Donaukastell Straubing – Sorviodurum**, Limesforschungen Band 3, Berlin.

Wallis Budge E.A. 1903   **An account of the Roman antiquities preserved in the museum at Chesters, Northumberland**, London.

Webster P.V. 1976   'Severn Valley Ware: a preliminary study', **Trans. Bristol & Glos. Arch. Soc.**, 94, 18-46.

Webster P.V. 1977   'Severn Valley Ware on the Antonine frontier', pp. 163–176 in J.Dore, K.Greene (Eds) **Roman pottery studies in Britain and beyond**, BAR, Suppl. ser., 30, Oxford.

Webster P.V. 1979   'Romano–British coarse pottery in the North–West', pp. 15–20 in N.J.Higham (Ed.) **The changing past**, Manchester.

Webster P.V. 1982   'Romano–British coarse pottery in North–West England. An introduction', **Lancs. Arch. J.**, 2, 13–31.

Wheeler R.E.M. 1926   **The Roman fort near Brecon**, Y Cymmrodor, 37, London.

Wild F. 1971   'The samian ware', pp.53–66 in G.D.B.Jones, 'Excavations at Northwich (Condate)', **Arch.J.**, 128, 31–77.

Wild F. 1975   'Samian ware', pp.141–177 in A.S.Robertson, **Birrens (Blatobulgium)**, Edinburgh.

Wild F. 1979   'Samian ware', pp. 269–291 in T.W.Potter, **Romans in North–West England**, Cumb. & Westmorland Ant. & Arch. Soc., Res. ser. 1. Kendal.

Williams D.F. 1977   'The Romano–British Black–burnished industry: an essay on characterisation by heavy mineral analysis', pp. 163–220 in D.P.S.Peacock (Ed.), **Pottery and early commerce**, London.

Woodward A.M.1926   'The Roman fort at Ilkley', **Yorks.Arch.J.**, 28, pts 2–3, 255 ff.